HAM RADIO SCHOOL.COM

VERE ADEPTO IS

HamRadioSchool.com

Technician License Course

*Complete Element 2 Exam Preparation
and more,
to help you really understand ham radio!*

by
Stu Turner
WØSTU

Second Edition: Version 2.4

Valid for NCVEC Technician Class Question Pool
July 1, 2014 to June 30, 2018

Acknowledgements: Tremendous thanks to the following for their time and assistance with this book and with *HamRadioSchool.com...* You guys rock!

James Bucknall, KDØMFO, for webmaster support, layout advice, graphics support, reviews, and great friendship!

Bob Witte, KØNR, for technical review, suggestions, educational support, web site contributions, photos, gear, and for being the Elmer Supreme!

Steve Galchutt, WGØAT, for web contributions, the SOTA thing, photos, and *goatly* inspiration! Tha-a-a-a-a-a-nks, Steve!

Paul Swanson, AAØK, for review, web contributions, equipment loans, photos, educational support, and classroom support! Thanks Paul!

Jürg Seyffer, KØPOP, for video support and hamfest marketing support.

Cole Turner, WØCOL, Jake Turner, WØJAK, and Emma Turner, for allowing me to unabashedly use their images in embarrassing harebrained graphics!

WØTLM Tri-Lakes Monument Radio Association, for being a great radio club and providing the opportunity to try a hand at instructing amateur radio courses!

KBØSA and Colorado BSA Troop 6, for the youthful enthusiasm for amateur radio and for motivational inspiration for this project! Go Scouts!

Liz, KTØLIZ, for putting up with the whole thing... again. Thanks honey!

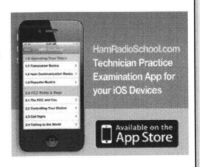

Teaching a ham class?

Check out our

Technician License Course Instructor's Charts!

Use our ready-to-teach book and charts and just add your Elmering wisdom, demo's, and exciting classroom activities for an easy-to-teach and successful Technician License class!

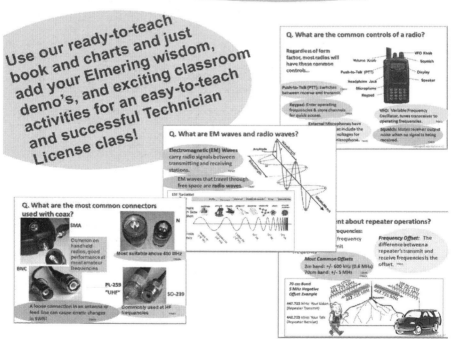

Fully coordinated with our book, section-by-section.
Loaded with colorful, instructional graphics.
Highlights all exam question pool items.
"Click-to-reveal" sequence of each chart's content.
Includes animations and imbedded audio.
Over 300 individual charts to guide your lessons.

Email: info@HamRadioSchool.com

You may also enjoy these recommended web sites and social media links:

HamRadioSchool.com Facebook Page:
> **https://www.facebook.com/hamradioschool**

HamRadioSchool.com on Twitter:
> **https://twitter.com/HamRadioSchool**

HamRadioSchool.com "Getting Started" links page:
> **http://www.HamRadioSchool.com/get_started**

> *Includes videos on setting up your first HT radio and other useful links!*

The KØNR Weblog:
> ***k0nr.com/blog***

KØNR Facebook Page:
> https://www.facebook.com/K0NRhamradio

The Goat Hiker:
> ***youtube.com/user/goathiker***

Summits On The Air (SOTA):
> ***na-sota.org***
> ***sota.org.uk***

Contents

Preface

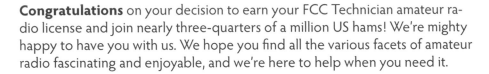

Congratulations on your decision to earn your FCC Technician amateur radio license and join nearly three-quarters of a million US hams! We're mighty happy to have you with us. We hope you find all the various facets of amateur radio fascinating and enjoyable, and we're here to help when you need it.

Why ham radio? Everyone has unique reasons for involvement with ham radio. Perhaps one of the most important is emergency preparation for your family. When an emergency arises – natural disasters like wildfire, tornados, hurricanes, earthquakes, or other man-made accidents or deliberate disruptions – cell phone networks are often overloaded or inoperative. Emergency responders are overwhelmed. Travel and access are frequently restricted. Throughout it all, ham radio remains operative and trustworthy, with robust, autonomous communication networks to keep you informed and to connect you with your family members when it really counts. This has been proven again and again around the world over decades of experience!

Many hams enjoy providing community service with their unique communications skills. Helping to coordinate and operate a parade, a foot or bicycle race, or a public community gathering with a group of fellow hams is an enjoyable and rewarding way to serve your community. Many hams also train and volunteer for deployment as public servants through emergency communications organizations that you will learn about in this book.

But for most amateur radio operators, ham radio is also a beloved hobby with a seemingly endless number of different aspects to investigate. From mountaintop peak operations to on-the-air group social gatherings to satellite and space station contacts to electronic circuit building to computer-digital communications to communicating around the globe, and much, much more, ham radio has an incredible array of activities to explore and enjoy. It can truly become a life-long hobby of fun and excitement for you and your family!

Is this book right for you? If you are interested in earning your Technician license, this book and its related web site are definitely for you, regardless of your background in science, technology, or math. If you have done nothing more than balance a checkbook since middle school math and you have replaced the batteries in an electronic toy, you are over-qualified to pass the Technician exam with help from this book and web site. If you are a professional engineer, a student of science, or a techno-whiz in your own right, you will likely speed through this book with enjoyment and enlightenment to license examination success in very short time.

Either way, this book will provide you fundamental understanding of radio along with the competence, and *confidence*, to get on the air with your first ham radio. Inside the book and on the web site you will find easy-to-grasp explanations of the technical topics using common examples and analogies to everyday things and experiences with which you are already familiar. You'll learn to use easy memory tricks and tools to help ensure your exam success. You will see ample pictures, graphics, and web-based multimedia that will help you intuitively comprehend everything from how radio electronics work to how to reach out and start a conversation on the air. You may even find it fun to read!

How is this book different? Unlike some other introductory ham radio books, this one does not pad its pages with the public domain questions from the exam question pool and try to "teach the test" by requiring you to memorize answers without understanding them. Rather, the pages are filled with relevant information that focuses you upon highlighted exam question content and that provides straightforward explanations so that you really comprehend radio. When you *really get it* you don't have to rely on mind-numbing memorization! Oh, and we provide you those public domain questions free, online at the *HamRadioSchool.com* web site, all organized by book section and accompanied by lots of additional content to help you learn very efficiently.

Yet other books are mind-numbingly technical and dry, filled with so much jargon and techno-speak that they seemingly require a Ph.D. in engineering to *really get it*. The goal of this book is to promote good, intuitive understanding of radio without *"going professorial"* on you. Simple explanations with a building-block approach will lead you to enjoyable learning, successful examination, and quickly getting on the air!

Get Going! Be sure you understand how to use this book as described in *Using This Book and Passing Your Exam* on the next page, and then start your learning both here and online at *HamRadioSchool.com*. If you have questions or comments for us, please contact us through the web site. We'll be glad to hear from you! *Good luck, and get going!*

With HamRadioSchool.com, passing your exam is easy.
More importantly, you'll *really get it!*
You'll really understand ham radio.
You'll be on the air quickly, with confidence!

Using This Book
and
Passing Your Exam

This *HamRadioSchool.com Technician License Course* book has been specially formatted to assist you with Technician license exam preparation! We recommend that you read this book's chapters in sequence first, then review material by topic, as necessary for your specific learning needs. We also recommend that you visit our web site, section-by-section, to take quizzes and to find additional materials that will make your learning experience an enjoyable one!

The *HamRadioSchool.com* web site provides additional learning tools organized section-by-section with the book. These enhanced learning tools may include video, audio, animations, graphics, photographs, or additional text explanations. You will also find the entire Technician Class exam question pool on the web site, with questions organized for ease of learning, section-by-section along with this book. You can also try out our quizzing and practice test app for mobile devices, containing all the quizzes and offering properly weighted practice exams anywhere, anytime. The combination of this book, the web-based learning tools, and the mobile app offers a powerful combination for really understanding ham radio.

Heavy Bold Text like this provides the answer to an exam pool question in *objective language* that mirrors the language of the question. All exam pool questions are covered this way in this book. The tab in the outer margin adjacent to the heavy bold text provides you the question identifier. You will find the exam questions and response options online, conveniently organized section-by-section, at *HamRadioSchool.com*. A page index of question identifiers is also included at the end of this book.

Example of Exam Question Objective Language Highlight and Exam Question:

Identification on the Air: **An amateur station is required to transmit its assigned call sign at least every 10 minutes during, and at the end of, a contact.**

T1F03

The margin tab identifies this as question T1F03. On the next page you will see the NCVEC question pool items T1F03 from which the boldface text above was derived. You'll find all the full exam pool questions at our web site for each section of this book.

T1F03 (D)   *Section 2.3, Page 41*
When is an amateur station required to transmit its assigned call sign?

    A. At the beginning of each contact, and every 10 minutes thereafter
    B. At least once during each transmission
    C. At least every 15 minutes during and at the end of a contact
    D. At least every 10 minutes during and at the end of a contact

We recommend that you read a book section, check for and review the section's online learning enhancements, and review the section's questions in exam pool format online or with our mobile app. As you get into later book chapters begin comprehensive practice tests online or with our app. When you are consistently passing practice exams you are ready for the real thing!

The Technician License (Element 2) Exam: The bottom line on passing the Technician exam is that you need at least 26 correct responses out of 35 total questions. That's about 74% correct answers to pass. There are 426 questions in the complete exam pool currently. Each question provides four multiple choice responses from which to choose. The order of the four question responses is not static -- their order will be scrambled on your exam among the "A B C D" designations.

Each exam will be comprised of questions drawn randomly from the exam pool, but with specific weighting applied by question topic. For example, the Technician exam must contain six exam questions from sub-element T1 that covers FCC rules, radio operator responsibilities, and related topics. The first two characters in a question's identifier specify its sub-element. The remaining exam weighting by sub-element are, with abbreviated descriptions:

T1	FCC Rules, Operator Responsibilities	6 questions
T2	Operating Procedures	3 questions
T3	Radio Waves and Propagation	3 questions
T4	Station Set Up & Practices	2 questions
T5	Electrical & Electronic Principles	4 questions
T6	Electrical & Electronic Components	4 questions
T7	Equipment, Problems, Troubleshooting	4 questions
T8	Modulation, Space Ops, Digital Modes	4 questions
T9	Antennas & Feedlines	2 questions
TØ	Safety	3 questions

The third character in the question identifier specifies a topical group of questions within each sub-element. Each sub-element may have several groups of questions. The last two characters in the identifier specify a question from the group. You will find descriptions of each sub-element and the groups within each sub-element online at *HamRadioSchool.com*, along with all of the exam pool questions.

The Exam Session: All amateur radio exams are administered by Volunteer Examiners (VE). A VE is a licensed ham who volunteers to help administer the tests and develop new licensed operators. A minimum of three VEs must administer every exam. VE sessions are conducted regularly in every state.

The exam is administered on paper and you will need a pencil (bring two, just in case one breaks), and you may use a calculator with any and all memories cleared. Take your time and RTFQ! That is, *Read The Fine Question* carefully! Your exam will be graded immediately by the VEs, so you'll know right away if you have passed. If you have used the *HamRadioSchool.com* learning system well, we're confident you will succeed the first time through! Good luck!

Amateur radio VE examination sessions are regularly held all over the country. The VE exam utilizes "fill in the circle" paper response sheets, and the fee is about $15. Volunteer Examiners are experienced hams who serve the amateur radio community by administering exams.

But, before we begin...

0.0 Before We Begin...

" *Have I done the world good, or have I added a menace? – Guglielmo Marconi*

Since you are investing time with this book I believe it is safe to assume that your response to Marconi regarding his invention, radio, would be something like, *"Good. Much good indeed!"* (Caution: Following amateur radio licensing some spouse's opinions may vary.) While he stood upon the shoulders of scientific giants such as Hertz, Maxwell, Faraday, Tesla and others, we all owe Marconi a great debt of gratitude for his insight and innovation conducted around the turn of the 20th Century. But this is not a history book, so let's get on with that for which you opened the cover. Let's start learning about amateur radio!

But before we begin getting into the testable material, take a look at the list of terms below. If you are comfortable with most of these terms and under-stand their meaning, you can probably just read this chapter's paragraphs on the *Amateur Bands* and *License Classes*, and then skip right to Chapter 1. Go ahead if you want, and the rest of us will catch up to you shortly. Of course, you're welcome to continue with us and review these basic technical subjects to make sure we have a solid, common understanding.

Electromagnetic Waves	Modulation
Frequency	Alternating Current
Wavelength	Voltage

If the terms above are new to you, you are uncertain of their meaning, or especially if they strike fear into your heart, please continue with this section! While each of these terms will be discussed in more depth later in the book it is important for readers who may not have a strong technical background to gain some fundamental knowledge of important technical topics in the easy-to-understand language and examples of this introductory chapter. Let's lay a solid foundation for these topics here, and the subsequent chapters' material will come much easier to you. Let's jump right into these terms.

Electromagnetic Waves: I am 100% certain that you have seen electromagnetic waves before. Light is comprised of a variety of electromagnetic waves that you perceive as various colors. These waves – we will call them EM waves for convenience – are made up of two different kinds of energy fields. As the name suggests, one of these energy fields is an *electric field* and the other is a *magnetic field*. You may have experienced an electric field by rubbing an inflated balloon on your hair to create a static charge that then pulls your hair toward the balloon. Every common magnet you have ever held creates a magnetic field that attracts many types of metal. All EM waves are made of those two kinds of invisible forces, or energy fields.

Why are they waves? The electric field and the magnetic field in EM transmissions vary in strength as they travel. Each energy field regularly increases and decreases in strength. We like to picture these fields rising and falling like water waves that are rolling along at the speed of light, as in Figure 0.1 below. As the wave travels past a stationary position, the electric field and the magnetic field smoothly increase and decrease in strength, or *amplitude*, as measured at the stationary position. Further, as indicated from the center axis of wave travel, the direction of each field reverses regularly, oscillating back-and-forth (up and down in the Figure 0.1) as observed from a stationary position. The distance the wave travels in one complete back-and-forth cycle is called the *wavelength*. You can imagine a wavelength as the distance from wave crest-to-crest, such as with a sequence of two regular ocean waves, or more conventionally where the axis of travel is crossed with one complete wave cycle.

Radio Waves: Like light, radio waves are EM waves too. They are different from light waves only in the rate at which their electric and magnetic fields

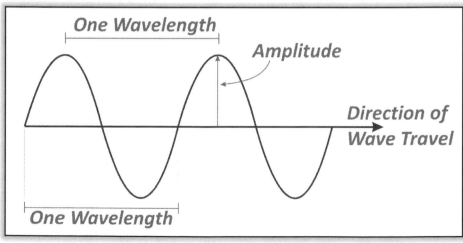

Figure 0.1: A Simple Electromagnetic Wave Model

wiggle back and forth as the wave travels past a stationary position. You may think of radio waves as being a bit lazier than light waves, wiggling the fields back-and-forth much slower than do light waves. But they still travel through space at the same speed as light waves, so that slower rate of wiggling makes for a lot longer distance covered in one of those back-and-forth cycles. In other words, radio waves have *longer wavelengths* than light waves.

Radio Frequency: The rate at which the electric field and magnetic field oscillate, stated as the number of completed cycles per second, is called the *frequency*. And remember, one back-and-forth cycle defines one wavelength of distance traveled. So frequency is also expressing the number of wavelengths per second that pass by as a continuous radio wave flies past you. The radio frequency to which you tune your radio – the radio in a car, the receiver of a stereo, or your new ham radio – is describing the number of cycles per second of the radio transmission. But instead of saying "cycles per second" all the time when discussing frequencies, we use the term *hertz* to mean cycles per second. Hertz is the unit of measure for radio frequency.

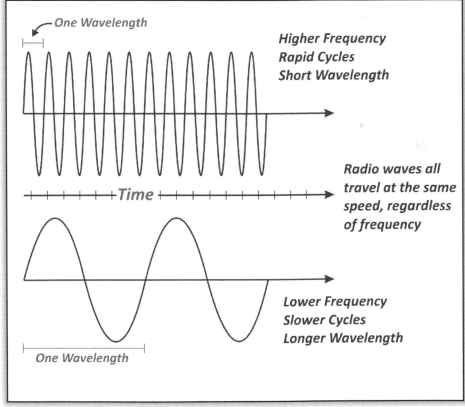

Figure 0.2: Comparison of Two EM Waves of Different Frequency

Modulation: *Modulation* is the process of placing an information signal into a radio wave by altering some characteristic of the wave. For example, we could simply turn the radio wave transmission on and off in distinct patterns to send a signal. *Morse Code signals* are like this, on and off patterns that represent letters, numbers, and punctuations. This modulation method is also called *continuous wave* (CW), because other characteristics of the waveform remain unchanged.

Instead of on-off patterns in the transmission we might change the frequency itself in a way that encodes a message. We could make the frequency shift higher or lower than a known reference frequency in patterns that carry a code of information. This is *frequency modulation*, or FM radio. The shifting FM frequencies often encode an audio voice signal, or music audio in the case of commercial FM radio.

We could vary the power level of the transmitted waves in a way that encodes a message. That is, we could manipulate the strength of the electric and magnetic fields as we transmit the wave. The energy level of the EM fields can be imagined as the height or size of the EM waves, and this is called the wave's *amplitude*. (Just like water waves, big tall waves have a lot of power, tiny short waves are weak!) Encoding a message by varying the EM field power or wave height is *amplitude modulation*, or AM radio. Again, the varying amplitude signal often will encode a voice audio signal. A special kind of AM used in

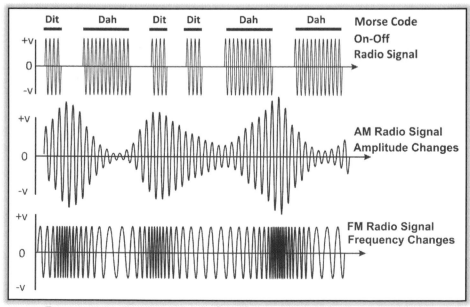

Figure 0.3: Comparison of Different Modulation Methods

amateur radio is called *single sideband* (SSB), and we'll discuss this more in Chapter 6.

In amateur radio we use different types of modulation, such as FM, AM, and SSB, to encode the sound of a voice or other forms of messages into the radio waves. Each modulation technique of sending a signal is called a *mode* of radio transmission.

Electrical Current: A radio transmitter uses electricity to produce radio waves. The way that electricity flows within wires or circuits, including antennas, helps to determine the frequency of the radio waves produced. Electricity is the movement of tiny charged particles called *electrons*. A measure of the amount of electrons moving through a wire is the *electrical current* – just like water current is a measure of the amount of water flowing down a river or through a pipe.

Voltage: *Voltage* is the force, or the pressure, pushing the electrons along through the wire. High voltage, like high water pressure, can really push the electrons forcefully through the wire in order that they can do a lot of work somewhere. Low voltage, like low water pressure, provides a less forceful push of the electrons along the wire. Also like water pressure in plumbing, voltage has a direction of force. It can push electrons this way or that in the wire, one direction or the other.

Direct and Alternating Current: When the voltage, or pressure, is pushing electrons in only one direction in a wire, we say that is *direct current* (DC). A typical battery produces one-way voltage resulting in direct current. However, other voltage sources such as the wall outlet of your home produce a constant back-and-forth pressure, effectively pushing-and-pulling the electrons in the wire. This kind of push-pull voltage creates *alternating current* (AC), with electrons accelerating in one direction in the wire, then slowing and reversing direction to accelerate the opposite way. This back-and-forth cycle of electron motion repeats continuously with alternating current, and we say that AC has a frequency of alternation, also expressed in hertz as the number of back-and-forth cycles per second.

Antenna Radiation: Notice that the back-and-forth current of AC is similar to the back-and-forth trading of energy in an EM radio wave. In fact, if you produce a rapidly alternating AC current – at rates equal to radio frequencies – and if you properly connect that AC current to an antenna, the antenna will convert the electrical energy into radio energy and radiate a radio wave with a frequency equal to the alternations of the AC electrical current. Radio frequency is determined by the AC frequency of back-and-forth electron motion

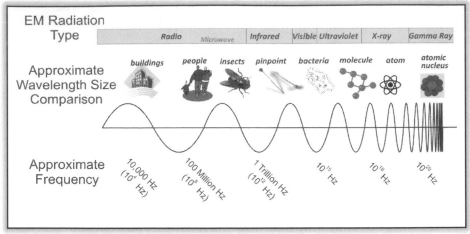

Figure 0.4: The Electromagnetic (EM) Spectrum

produced in a radio's electronic circuitry. An electrically energized antenna radiating radio frequency EM waves is somewhat like the electrically energized filament of a light bulb radiating visible EM waves of light.

EM Spectrum: The entire range of EM frequencies is very wide, and radio frequencies (RF) are on the low end of the range. In other words, in the spectrum of EM waves from radio waves to light waves to X-rays, RF has the slowest rates of EM field oscillations, and that also means the longest wavelengths. As EM frequency gets higher, the wavelengths get shorter and we move out of radio waves and up into light waves. The even higher frequencies with their very short wavelengths take us up into X-ray and Gamma Ray territory.

RF Spectrum: The radio frequencies include EM radiation up to a few hundred billion hertz. That is some mighty fast EM oscillation cycles, huh? Hundreds of billions of cycles every second! Most of the frequencies we will discuss for amateur radio use will be a few million to a few hundred million hertz. We will use the prefix "mega" to mean million, so megahertz (MHz) means "millions of cycles per second."

Scientists and engineers have named the different broad ranges of radio frequencies with some quite general names that you've probably heard before. In this amateur radio book we will be interested primarily in these frequency ranges:

High Frequency (HF): 3 to 30 MHz
Very High Frequency (VHF): 30 to 300 MHz
Ultra High Frequency (UHF): 300 to 3000 MHz

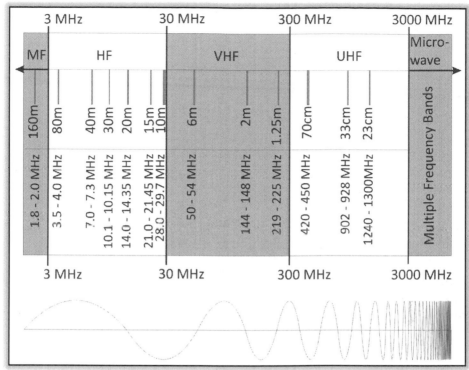

Figure 0.5: Amateur Radio Bands Within HF, VHF, and UHF Ranges

Amateur Bands: Within each of those very broad categories of HF, VHF, and UHF, several specific little ranges, or *bands*, of frequencies are reserved by law for amateur radio use. You may imagine each of these bands as being just like the commercial FM radio band that ranges from about 88 MHz to 108 MHz, and you can tune your radio across the band to pick up individual stations at different frequencies within the band. Compared to the entire radio spectrum these amateur bands are rather small, but they each contain from a few hundred thousand to a few tens of millions of hertz worth of frequencies, or *bandwidth.*

These amateur radio bands are identified by the frequency range they cover, but they are more commonly named by ham operators as the *approximate wavelength* of the band. Although each specific frequency in the band produces a slightly different wavelength, all of the band's wavelengths are "in the ballpark" near a rounded wavelength value that is used as the name of the band. For example, we will speak of the 10 meter band to identify radio frequencies from 28.0 to 29.7 MHz, all of which produce wavelengths that are near 10 meters (about 30 feet) in length.

Amateur License Classes: Currently only three different classes of amateur radio licenses are awarded in the United States: *Technician, General,* and *Extra.* The introductory license class is Technician and the highest available license class is Extra. As a radio operator progresses from Technician, to General, to Extra, more of the amateur radio bands are available to the license holder. The Technician is allowed to transmit on all bands in the UHF and VHF ranges, as well as limited segments and limited modes on some of the bands in the HF range. General class license holders are permitted to transmit by all modes on all Technician allocations plus large segments of each band in the HF range. Extra license holders have no restrictions, permitted to transmit on all amateur radio bands and with all modes. (Within established guidelines for use.)

Grandfathered License Classes: In earlier years the classes of amateur licenses and band privileges were parsed more finely, and six license classes were awarded in the US from 1978 to 2000. An introductory license with band privileges lower than Technician was called *Novice.* Above Technician was *Technician Plus.* Between General and Extra was a license class called *Advanced.* Although Novice and Advanced licenses are no longer granted, they are grandfathered classes, and many ham operators still hold these licenses and the band privileges that are associated with them. No Technician Plus licenses are held any longer by current FCC-licensed operators.

Now that you have a basic understanding of some radio-related technical topics, you are ready to begin your Technician license preparation. You will see each of those terms and topics again as you read through the book, along with some alternate descriptions of these concepts and some additional information about amateur radio operations. Be sure you have reviewed the *"Using This Book"* information in the introduction, then move on to Chapter 1.0 and start becoming a ham radio operator!

1.0   Operating Your Radio

❝ *Let's talk about the radio...*
— Fern Moyse
[The Hackensaw Boys]

Yes, let's talk about the radio, as Fern suggests! After all, that's why we're here.

In this chapter you will learn the practical basics necessary for the operation of any ham radio. In Section 1.1 we will cover a transceiver's common controls and components and introduce you to the different modes of transmitting and receiving signals. Section 1.2 is a summary of ham radio communication basics, including some common on-the-air procedures and terms, as well as an overview of the most common problems new hams have and how to solve them. Section 1.3 is all about amateur radio repeater stations and how you can use them to extend your radio's communications range. Ready?

Let's talk, starting with that new transceiver you're anxious to get.

1.1   Operating Your Radio
Transceiver Basics

Modern ham radios are a combination of a transmitter and a receiver, called a *transceiver*. A transmitter emits radio waves to carry your signal out to the world, while a receiver captures others' radio signals so you can hear them. **A transceiver** is a unit that does both jobs, **combining the functions of a transmitter and receiver,** and allowing easy two-way radio communication with one device.

All transceivers have some common basic parts.

Microphone: Converts sound into electrical signals, or audio signals, for the transmitter.

Transmitter: Encodes audio signals into radio frequency emissions. This encoding process is called *modulation.*

Antenna: Radiates radio frequency emissions during transmissions and detects radio frequencies during reception.

Receiver: Converts, or *demodulates,* radio signals back into audio signals.

Speaker: Transforms audio electrical signals into sounds.

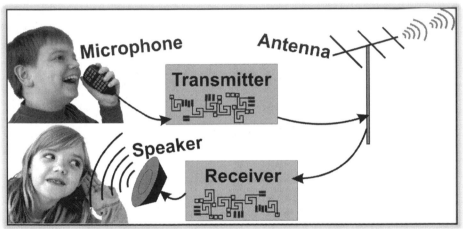

Figure 1.1: Transceiver Basic Components

Transceivers are manufactured in many sizes and forms, but most modern amateur transceivers fit into one of three common types.

Handheld Transceiver (HT): The HT radio is commonly the first type of ham radio that a Technician licensee will own. It is a small radio that fits in your hand and contains an integrated battery, an integrated antenna, and an integrated microphone. Although limited in output power it is very useful for portable communications. HTs usually transmit only *frequency modulated* (FM) signals in the VHF and/or UHF frequency ranges only. **A handheld transceiver may be linked to an RF power amplifier to increase low power output.**

Mobile Station: A medium sized radio that typically uses either automobile battery power or a separate AC power supply. Mobile radios use an external antenna connected with coaxial cable and a separate handheld microphone. These radios are commonly installed in automobiles, but they may also be

T7A10

Figure 1.2: Transceiver Form Factor Types

used in homes as small base stations. Mobiles provide higher output power than HT radios, and some more capable models provide multiple operational modes and multiple frequency bands (Modes: FM, SSB, AM; Bands: HF/VHF/UHF).

Base Station: Larger in size and typically using an AC power supply or an extensive DC battery bank, these radios require external cable-connected antenna(s) and a separate handheld or desk microphone. A modern base station transceiver will usually provide higher output power and is frequently coupled with a separate component power amplifier. These radios typically provide multiple operational modes and multiple frequency bands. (Modes: FM, SSB, AM, CW; Bands: HF/VHF/UHF).

You probably noticed that some of these transceiver types offer multiple operational *modes* and *bands.* You may be wondering what that means. The start-up Chapter 0.0 provided some insight about modes and bands, and we'll learn more about amateur radio bands in Section 4.2, but let's get right to this matter of modes again. It's quite simple really!

Mode refers to the method of modulating a radio signal, or encoding information into the radio signal. So, the mode is the particular way that your voice (or other type of information) is put into the radio signal that your radio transmits. This is done by varying some characteristic of the radio waves with the variations of your voice, or other information type.

Let's just get introduced to some common ham radio modes for now. We'll examine these more closely in later chapters.

FM: *Frequency Modulation.* Frequency is the number of radio waves (cycles) per second a transmitter emits. In frequency modulation, small variations are made in the emitted radio frequencies that mirror the sound variations of your voice in the audio input signal. **FM is the mode most commonly used with VHF and UHF phone (voice) communications, including voice repeater stations that relay your signals. FM is also commonly used for VHF packet radio (digital) communications.**

AM: *Amplitude Modulation.* Every radio wave has a level of power, or wave height, known as the wave's *amplitude.* With AM, the power level of the emitted radio wave is varied to encode your voice audio signal (or other type of information) into the radio transmission.

SSB: *Single Sideband* mode is a special type of AM. The very efficient **SSB mode is often used for long distance or weak signal contacts on the VHF and UHF bands,** and it is very common on HF bands. **The primary advantage of SSB over FM for voice transmissions is narrower bandwidth,** meaning that a smaller portion of available radio spectrum is used. In other words, a smaller range or number of frequencies is necessary to carry the voice audio information. We'll examine more on bandwidth and sidebands in Section 6.3.

CW: *Continuous Wave* means that the transmitted signal is unchanging. No FM or AM modulation varies the signal. Rather, the signal transmission itself is interrupted in patterns over time to encode information. Morse Code is by far the most common code used by hams in CW mode. With Morse Code patterns of on/off radio transmissions represent letters, numbers, and punctuations.

Other modes are used by hams, particularly with a computer connected to the radio to create *digital signals* or to transmit images. We'll dig into that awesomeness a little later in Chapter 10.

Transceiver Controls: You may have seen some ham radios, or at least you have seen the examples in the pictures of this section, and you may be wondering what all those knobs and dials and buttons do and what other compo-

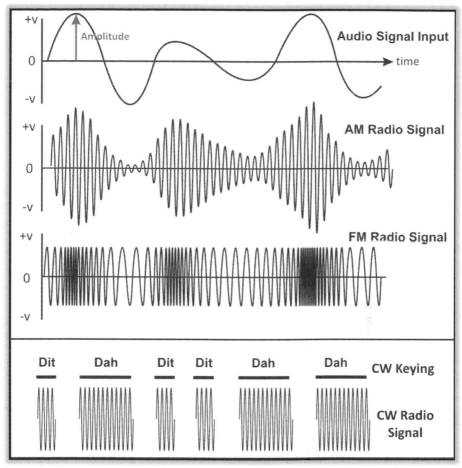

Figure 1.3: Modulation Methods

nents you may need to get on the air. Here are some basics about controls and components that will help you get started understanding your radio.

Push-To-Talk (PTT): The PTT button on a microphone or the side of an HT radio is used exactly that way -- You literally push to talk! Pushing the PTT button activates the microphone and radio transmitter, sending your signal to the world. **PTT switches between receive and transmit. (Note: External microphones on amateur radio transceivers use connectors that include the push-to-talk signal and voltages for powering the microphone.)**

Squelch: This control mutes the receiver output noise when no signal is being received. Commonly a rotary knob control, you can adjust the signal strength required to *open the squelch* and allow the receiver to create audio for you to hear. The squelch control cuts out random noise that you don't want to listen to in between radio transmissions.

T7A07 T4A01

T4B03

Variable Frequency Oscillator (VFO): This is the tuning control for your radio, used to scroll and **tune the transceiver to operating frequencies.** The VFO control is typically a rotary knob and may also be coupled with up/down arrow keys on a keypad. You will learn in Chapter 6 why it has that strange name.

Keypad: Most modern radios, particularly HTs, include an **integrated keypad with which you may enter operating frequencies, store favorite frequencies in channels to enable quick access,** program repeater channels and tones, and vary the functions of your radio. Modern radios may have multiple menu levels to control a wide variety of functions and set up features, and the keypad is the key to them all.

Headphones: Most radios support the use of headphones in place of a regular speaker. Headphones can help you copy signals in noisy areas, and most radios have connection ports for combination headphones-microphone assemblies. Some of these assemblies provide voice activated microphones, or *VOX,* in which PTT is activated by the relatively strong sound of your voice rather than a push-button.

Power Sources: Most HT radios will use an integrated battery that must be recharged or replaced over time. Larger radios commonly use **a regulated power supply (AC power supply) that will prevent voltage fluctuations from reaching sensitive circuits.** However, almost all ham radios can be powered by external battery sources, and many hams keep a bank of back-up batteries on hand for emergency operations during power outages.

Antennas: Most HT radios are sold with a short integrated antenna referred to as a 'Rubber Duck' due to its rubberized molded exterior. **The Rubber Duck antenna does not transmit or receive as effectively as a full sized antenna, and its signals will be significantly weaker if used inside a car** where the surrounding metal will block signals. Larger radios will typically use external antennas that are sold separately from the radio. You may easily connect your HT to an external antenna by removing the rubber duck antenna and using coaxial cable and compatible connectors. Longer HT-mounted antennas for improved performance of handhelds are readily available also, supplanting the shorter rubber duck.

A great combination for the new ham is an HT radio and a magnetically mounted automobile roof antenna connected with a narrow cable that can slip through the door or window seal. That way you can connect your HT to the car external antenna for significantly improved performance when on the road, and use your rubber duck when on foot! *Quack, quack!*

Congratulations! You have completed your first step toward your FCC amateur radio Technician License!

Now go to the *HamRadioSchool.com* web site and review the related questions from the technician question pool for **Section 1.1**.

www.HamRadioSchool.com/tech_media

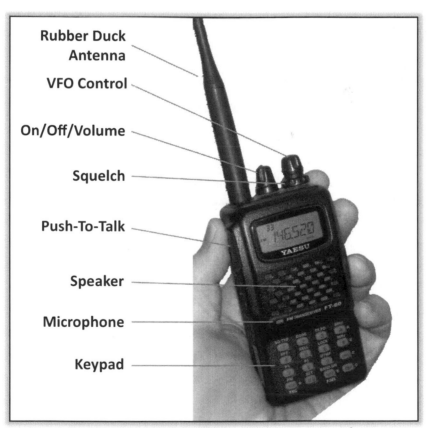

Figure 1.4: Typical HT Transceiver Controls

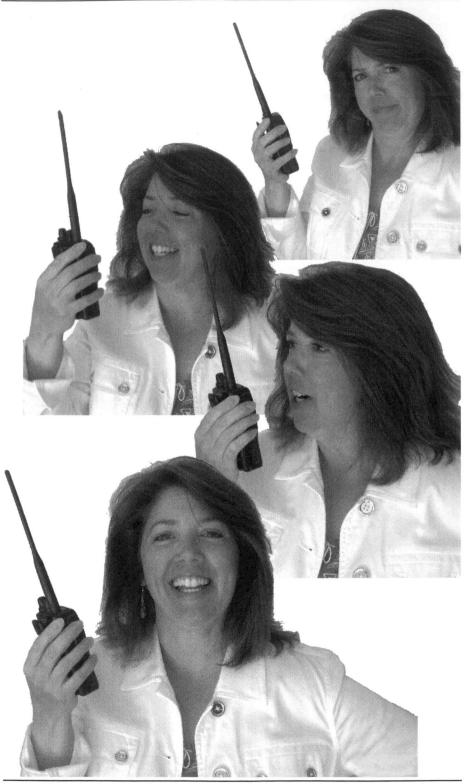

1.2 Operating Your Radio
Ham Communication Basics

❝ *The public airwaves provide a chance to affirm we want to be a good, decent people; a good, decent nation. — Charles W. Pickering*

You've got your license and new radio, you've got the transceiver control basics figured out, and you are ready to get on the air! What now? What do you say? How do you reach out to another ham? What frequency do you use? What cool ham phrases or terms should you use?

Don't worry, it's easy, and the ham radio community is jam packed with friendly folks – good, decent people – who will be happy to help a new operator get started. If you haven't been around ham radio very much and have not heard others talking on the air, it's probably a good idea to find a popular repeater station and just listen for a while. Then, when you're ready, use that PTT and make your first call! Here are some basic pointers to get your on-the-air communications off to a stellar beginning!

Simplex Communications: Transmitting and receiving on the same, singular frequency, directly from radio to radio (as contrasted with repeater communications.) Your local area likely has coordinated specific frequencies for simplex communications on the VHF and UHF bands, and you should stick to these standard channels to help reduce interference. Ask an experienced ham about your local coordinated band plan, or use the national calling frequencies first to attempt to contact others in your area.

`T2B01`

Repeater Communications: A repeater amateur station receives your signal on one channel (frequency) **and simultaneously re-transmits it on a different channel.** So, repeater communications use more than one frequency: One frequency for transmitting and one frequency for listening. The repeater station is always the relay between you and others whom you may not be able to reliably reach by simplex communication. Your radio can be programmed to automatically switch from the repeater's "listen to" frequency to its "transmit to" or "talk" frequency when you PTT. That way, the practical use of repeaters is not much different from simplex operations. You will learn more about repeaters next in Section 1.3.

`T1F09`

Station Identification: An amateur operator must properly identify with call sign for any transmission, even brief

`T2A06`

Figure 1.5: Simplex vs. Repeater Communications

transmissions to test equipment or antennas, identifying every 10 minutes and at the end of any set of transmissions.

CQ Contact: **The procedural signal CQ means "calling any station."** More commonly used with noisier weak signal SSB communications than on FM repeaters or simplex, the CQ call will typically be repeated two or three times followed by the calling station's call sign. **A station responding to a CQ call should repeat the other station's call sign followed by its own call sign.**

When choosing an operating frequency for calling CQ, listen first to be sure no one else is using the frequency. You may also ask if the frequency is in use. Make sure you are in your assigned band as well, within your license privileges (see Section 4.2).

Specific Station Contact: **When you are calling a specific station whose call sign you know, you simply say the other station's**

Transmit your FCC call sign every 10 minutes and at the end of any set of transmissions!

While there is no requirement to identify your station at the start of a set of transmissions, most operators do that also.

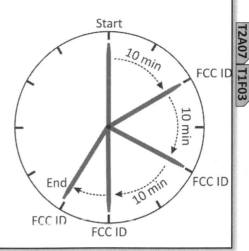

Figure 1.6: FCC Station Identification Requirements

call sign then identify with your own call sign. This applies to simplex and repeaters.

National Calling Frequencies: Standard frequencies on VHF and UHF bands reserved for making initial simplex contact with other stations. Once contact is established the communicating stations should move to another frequency in order to keep the calling frequency open for all stations' use.

2 meter band: 146.520 MHz is the national FM calling frequency.
70 cm band: **446.000 MHz is the national calling frequency.**

Q-Signals: Abbreviations derived from Morse Code operations that are commonly used even in phone (voice) communications. Q-Signals help keep transmissions brief and efficient, and they are widely used by hams. A full list of Q-Signals is available on *HamRadioSchool.com*, but common Q-Signals include:

QRM: Interference from other radio stations
QRN: Static interference or atmospheric noise
QRP: Using low power; shall I reduce power?
QRQ: Send more quickly, send faster (CW speed)
QRS: Send more slowly (CW speed)
QRZ: Who is calling me?
QSL: Acknowledge receipt
QSO: A radio contact or conversation
QSY: Change of frequency

QTH: Location; what is your location?

73: Best regards (A procedural sign, not a Q-Signal, but commonly used)

T2B08

Common Courtesy: No single radio amateur has sole privilege or rights to any amateur frequency, and common courtesy should prevail when two stations transmitting on the same frequency interfere with each other. If your station's transmission unintentionally interferes with another station, properly identify and move to a different frequency. Often a club or organization will have regularly scheduled on-air meetings called "nets," particularly on repeaters. Use common courtesy and move to another repeater or another frequency in such cases, and better yet, become familiar with the club and net schedules on repeaters that you use so that you may plan your use around scheduled events on the air. Even better still, inquire about joining in on nets of interest to you!

Self-Regulating Service: The amateur radio service prides itself on being a self-regulated, self-policed service under the FCC. As a licensed operator you should know the rules and follow them, encourage other operators in a positive way to uphold the same standards, and take pride in your on-air operations, making them efficient, enjoyable, and friendly.

Common Problems & Solutions: As you gain some experience with ham radio you will encounter some of the following common problems that limit or diminish your radio's performance. Most of these common problems have easy solutions. Let's wrap up this section with a look at eight common problems and how to solve them.

T3C11 T3C10

1. Radio Horizon: **The distance over which two stations can communicate by direct path.** This distance is somewhat further than the visual horizon, or visual line-of-sight, **because the earth seems less curved to radio waves than to light waves.** That is, radio waves

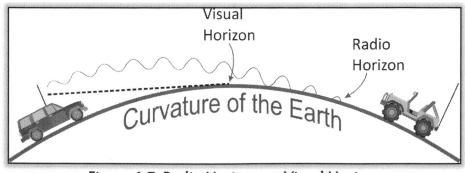

Figure 1.7: Radio Horizon vs. Visual Horizon

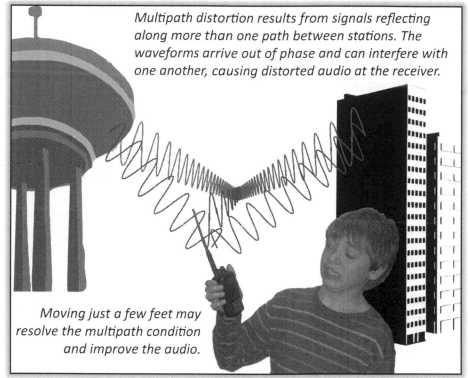

Multipath distortion results from signals reflecting along more than one path between stations. The waveforms arrive out of phase and can interfere with one another, causing distorted audio at the receiver.

Moving just a few feet may resolve the multipath condition and improve the audio.

Figure 1.8: Multipath Distortion and Random Reflections

are bent over the horizon a little more by the atmosphere and ground effects than are light waves. VHF and UHF signals are usually limited by the radio horizon, but repeater stations at a distance or in high locations help to resolve this limitation.

2. **Inside Buildings: UHF frequencies** (70 cm band) **are often more effective than VHF frequencies** (2m band) **inside buildings because the shorter UHF wavelengths allow for easier penetration of building structure.**

3. Intermittent Signals: **If another operator reports that your station's signals were strong a moment ago but are now weak or distorted, you may be experiencing random reflections and multi-path distortion.** In this situation your signal travels by more than one path to the receiving station and with varying distances or wave phase relationships among the signals. **Moving just a few feet** may resolve the reflections and improve your transmitted signal or your received signal if you are experiencing distortion in your audio. Inside buildings where many materials such as pipes and wires are inside walls,

floors, and ceilings, moving just a few feet will often improve your signal if it is blocked or reflected by these hidden metal objects.

4. **Picket Fencing: A rapid fluttering sound that is commonly heard from mobile stations that are moving while transmitting.** This is common with automobiles moving rapidly near metal signs, bridges, buildings, or other features in the environment that block or reflect the radio signals.

5. **Obstructions:** Buildings, hills, or other natural or man-made features may block your direct line of sight path to a distant repeater or other station. **A directional antenna may be used to try and find a path that reflects your signals to the other station.** The directional antenna will allow you to focus most of the transmitted energy in the direction of the reflection path, thereby improving your signal strength along that indirect path.

6. Antenna Polarization: The physical orientation of both your antenna and the radio waves it emits. All electromagnetic (EM) waves, including radio waves, have a definite direction of oscillation of the intensity of electrical and magnetic fields that make up the wave, and that direction changes with your antenna's orientation. Specifically, **the orientation of the electric field of a radio wave is used to describe its polarization.**

   a. **Identical polarization of the transmitting and receiving stations is best for signal strength,** usually either vertical antenna orientation or horizontal antenna orientation, **else signals will be significantly weaker.** (We will elaborate on this more in later sections.)

   b. **Vertical polarization**, where your antenna is vertical, is most common for FM simplex and FM repeater operations. Hold your HT antenna straight vertical for the best performance. The electric field oscillations will be vertical to the earth's surface, expanding and contracting up and down during each wave cycle.

   c. **Horizontal polarization, where your antenna elements are horizontal, is common for long-distance weak-signal operations using the VHF and UHF bands, particularly with CW and SSB modes.** The electric field oscillation is horizontal to the earth.

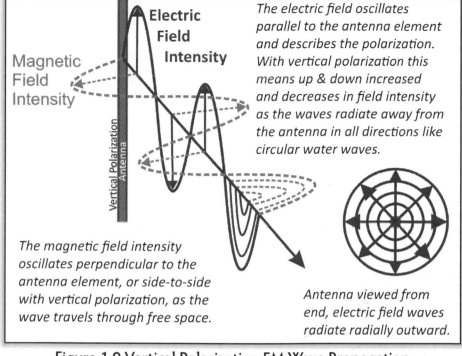

The electric field oscillates parallel to the antenna element and describes the polarization. With vertical polarization this means up & down increased and decreases in field intensity as the waves radiate away from the antenna in all directions like circular water waves.

The magnetic field intensity oscillates perpendicular to the antenna element, or side-to-side with vertical polarization, as the wave travels through free space.

Antenna viewed from end, electric field waves radiate radially outward.

Figure 1.9 Vertical Polarization EM Wave Propagation

7. **Over Deviating:** Your FM signal is being driven too hard by your microphone's audio signal, causing distortion. **Talk farther away from the microphone if you are told your FM transceiver is over deviating.** `T7B01`

8. **Distorted or Unintelligible Signals:** This can be caused by several factors including **your transmitter being slightly off frequency, your batteries running low, or simply being in a bad location.** `T7B10`

There you go! With these basics of ham communication under your belt you'll be ready to get on the air. Take a look at the related Technician test questions on **HamRadioSchool.com** for **Section 1.2**. I'll bet you can get most of them correct already!

www.HamRadioSchool.com/tech_media

Summary Table of Eight Common Problems / Solutions

1.	Radio horizon blocks VHF/UHF signals and is the distance over which two stations can communication by direct path, but it is somewhat beyond the visual horizon (the earth seems less curved to radio waves).
2.	UHF frequencies penetrate building structures more easily than VHF frequencies, so UHF works better inside buildings.
3.	Multipath distortion and random reflections may be solved by moving your position just a few feet.
4.	Picket fencing is a fluttering noise often heard from mobile stations.
5.	You may be able to transmit "around" obstructions using a directional antenna to bounce signals off of terrain or structures.
6.	Polarization is the direction of electric field oscillations in the EM wave, and the best communications are with all stations having identical polarization, else your signals will be weak.
7.	Over deviating is when the audio signal is too strong, causing distortion in the modulated RF signal and received audio. Talk further away from the microphone to resolve over deviation.
8.	Distortion or unintelligible signals may be caused by a slightly off-frequency transmitter, low batteries, or poor location.

Operating Your Radio
1.3   **Repeater Basics**

❝ *There is no harm in repeating a good thing. — Plato*

Y ou have made your first simplex contact and a friendly fellow ham told you about a really cool repeater nearby on which a local group holds a new ham discussion net every Thursday night. That's exactly the kind of forum you'd like to get involved with! So, how do you get onto that repeater? How do you set up your radio for it? What are the QSOs like on a repeater?

Once again, the answers to these questions are not cosmic or complicated. A repeater is a good thing, so let's see how to utilize it.

Repeater: An amateur radio station that simultaneously re-transmits the signal of another amateur station on a different channel or channels. Repeaters are often located on high terrain, on tall buildings, or on high towers, and they may retransmit at relatively high power levels, so the originating station's signal may be relayed over a much larger distance than is possible with the originating station alone.

T1F09

Frequency Offset: The difference between a repeater's trans-mit and receive frequencies. All stations will monitor a repeater on its transmit frequency (your "listen" frequency). All stations will transmit to a repeater on its receive frequency (your "talk" frequency). Thus, when you use your "talk" frequency your signal is instantly repeated on the "listen" frequency for all other stations to hear. The difference between these two frequencies is the repeater *frequency offset*.

T4B11

When you program a repeater channel into your radio, you'll select the proper offset value for the specific repeater.

- o **Positive Offset:** Your talk frequency is higher than your listen fre-quency. (The repeater's receive is higher than its transmit.)

- o **Negative Offset:** Your talk frequency is lower than your listen fre-quency. (The repeater's receive is lower than its transmit.)

Figure 1.10: Example of Repeater Offset Frequencies and Tones

T2A03 | T2A01

- o **2m Band Offset: The most common 2m offset is 600 kHz (0.6 MHz), either positive or negative.**

- o **70cm Band Offset: The most common 70cm offset is 5 MHz, either positive or negative.**

When you program a repeater channel into your radio with an offset value it will automatically shift to the required "talk" frequency when you PTT. Most modern radios have the standard repeater offset values for the United States pre-programmed, including standards for positive or negative offset according to the portion of a band being utilized. However, not all US locations adhere to these standards and you may have to override the pre-programmed values to properly set up some repeater channels.

Tones and Squelch: Many repeaters require the use of a sub-audible tone in your transmission to activate the repeater. Although the tone is there and the repeater receives it, you do not hear it. If there is no tone in your transmission the repeater will ignore you! The tone is required to open the squelch of the repeater's receiver and allow your signal to be "heard" by the repeater. And there are other types of tones sometimes used for the same purpose, as listed on the opposite page.

When you program a repeater frequency pair into a radio channel you'll select the proper tone to be transmitted each time you push-to-talk, in addition to the offset value. The following is a summary of the various tone types that may be used to properly access a repeater, and a couple of related items about repeaters:

CTCSS: Continuous Tone-Coded Squelch System. This is the most common tone system used in the US, and it is also referred to as "PL Tone." **CTCSS**

uses the sub-audible tone transmitted with normal voice audio to open the squelch of the receiver. There are 42 standard CTCSS tone frequencies. [T2B02]

DCS: Digital Coded Squelch uses a stream of digital data to open the receiver's squelch.

Tone Burst: More common in Europe, a transmission of a 1,750 Hz audio tone at the beginning of each transmission used to open the receiver's squelch.

If a repeater receiver requires a CTCSS tone, DCS tone sequence, or an audio tone burst, you might be able to hear but not access the repeater even when transmitting with the proper offset frequency. [T2B04]

Carrier Squelch: Only a radio frequency (RF) signal is required to break the squelch. The simplest type of squelch based on the presence or absence of a signal, this is the same as the basic squelch circuit of your radio. **Muting controlled solely by the presence or absence of an RF signal is called carrier squelch.** [T2B03]

Courtesy Tones: With repeaters you will often hear tones inserted by the repeater at the end of a repeated transmission. These courtesy tones have no squelch affect and are simply to help identify when another user has ended a transmission. And they sound cool!

Open/Closed Repeaters: By using tone squelch or other activation methods, some repeaters may be closed to public amateur use and reserved for only emergency, organizational, or club use. The majority of repeaters are open to use by all licensed amateurs. A good source of repeater information, including open/closed status, offset frequencies, and tone requirements, is a published repeater directory or an online description from the repeater operators.

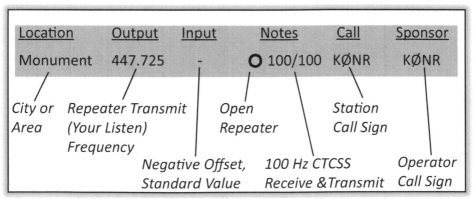

Figure 1.11: Sample Repeater Directory Listing

T2A09 **T2A04**

Calling for Contact: On repeaters, the CQ call is rarely used. Rather, **to indicate that you are listening and interested in a contact simply transmit your call sign.** As with simplex communication, if you know the call sign of another specific station you wish to call via a repeater, **say the other station's call sign then identify with your call sign.**

T1A09 **T1A08**

Repeater Coordination is conducted by regional **frequency coordinators** who are **selected by amateur operators in the local or regional area whose stations are eligible to be repeater or auxiliary stations. The coordinator recommends transmit/receive channels and other parameters for repeaters and auxiliary stations** to minimize interference between these stations and to ensure the most efficient use of the radio spectrum.

Linked Repeaters: Repeaters may be linked together using auxiliary stations or by other methods. Linked repeater systems involving many repeater stations can provide very broad coverage of VHF and UHF signals. When using a linked repeater you should be aware that your transmissions may be carried over a wide area and you should first research the usage policies established by the repeater system operators. In many cases linked repeater systems have policies of no "rag chewing," or extended casual conversations, in order that the wide area coverage system remain available for higher priority or emergency messages.

T2B12

Simplex Instead? When stations can communicate directly without using a repeater, the operators should consider communicating via simplex rather than a repeater. You can easily check whether or not simplex communication is possible, and some radios have a special convenient control to momentarily swap the transmit and receive pairs of a repeater memory channel. This way you can momentarily monitor the other stations' direct transmissions to hear if simplex communication is possible and, if so, free the repeater for others to use.

Spectacular! Now you can dig into your radio's user manual, read the specifics of how to set up a repeater channel, and understand exactly what you are doing and what all the frequencies and tones are about. Repeater communications are fun and convenient, and you'll be using repeaters in no time.

Now, let's see what the exam question pool has in store for you regarding repeaters. Hit the Technician pool questions for **Section 1.3.**

www.HamRadioSchool.com/tech_media

2.0 FCC Rules & Regs

> **You have to learn the rules of the game. And then you have to play better than anyone else. — Albert Einstein**

Now you're radiating! Really, you're transmitting on repeaters, communicating simplex, and having a blast on the air. But, what rules do you have to follow regarding your transmissions? Are there things you cannot say on the air? Can you let your little brother talk on your ham radio, or Uncle Fred who has no license? Can you take your radio on vacation to Europe and transmit? And what about your license? How long does it last? Do you have to retest in the future? So many questions! But all the answers are right here. Don't fret.

This chapter is all about THE RULES. As a licensed amateur radio operator you are responsible for understanding and playing by the rules and regulations established by the **Federal Communications Commission (FCC), the agency that regulates and enforces the rules for the Amateur Radio Service in the United States.** Let's start *learning the rules of the game* with the relationship between the FCC and you that your amateur radio license will establish. `T1A02`

2.1 The FCC and You

FCC Rules & Regs

Amateur Radio Service: The FCC sanctions the Amateur Radio Service for persons who are interested in radio technique solely with a personal aim and without pecuniary interest (that is, without profit or money-making intent). **One purpose of the Amateur Radio Service stated in FCC regulations is to advance skills in the technical and communication phases of the radio art.** In the spirit of this purpose, **a permissible use of the Amateur Radio Service is allowing a person to conduct radio experiments and to communicate with other licensed hams around the world.** `T1A01` `T1A12`

T1A03 **Part 97: The FCC rules and regulations that govern the Amateur Radio Service are contained in FCC Regulation Part 97.** There are many sub-parts to Part 97 that provide guidelines on virtually every aspect of amateur radio. While Part 97 provides much spellbinding reading, it is not necessary for you to memorize it to become a ham radio operator. Simply be familiar with the most commonly applicable Part 97 rules and know that you can find guidance in Part 97 when you begin to venture beyond the typical **T2C01** amateur operations. However, be aware that **the FCC rules always apply to the operation of an amateur station** licensed by the FCC.

T1A10 **Amateur Station: Part 97 defines an amateur station as a station in an Amateur Radio Service consisting of the apparatus necessary for carrying on radio communications.** Well, that's pretty obvious, huh? By this definition a simple HT transceiver is an amateur station. So is that mobile unit installed in an automobile.

Rules Under Part 97: Most of the FCC part 97 rules are not hard to learn and are easy to comply with. The following list of SEVEN BIG RULES provides the most commonly applicable rules to amateur stations and operators. Learn them, know them, live them:

T1F13 1. **FCC Inspection: You must make your station and records available to FCC inspection any time upon request by an FCC representative.** Inspections very rarely occur. Usually an FCC inspection will be initiated only in cases of repeated rules violations by a station. Rules violations are usually reported by other responsible amateur operators when violations occur multiple times with a known station. Additionally, the *American Radio Relay League* (ARRL) operates the *amateur auxiliary*, a volunteer organization that works in conjunction with the FCC to monitor activity on amateur radio frequencies and encourage amateur operators to self-police.

T1C07 2. **Mailing Address:** You must provide and maintain a correct mailing address with the FCC for document receipt. **If correspondence is returned as undeliverable to the FCC your license may be revoked or suspended.**

 3. **Minimum Necessary Power: Under normal, non-distress circumstances, an amateur should use the minimum transmitter power necessary to carry out the desired communication while not exceeding the maximum power permitted.** This is difficult to judge sometimes, but as you learn you'll become comfortable with adjusting your radio power and requesting signal reports from other operators to better comply with this rule.

4. **Prohibited Activities:** The FCC, the *ARRL amateur auxiliary*, and most amateur operators don't take well to the following six prohibited activities:

a. **Indecent or obscene words or language are prohibited in amateur transmissions.** There is no official list of prohibited foul terms, but you will probably know them if you hear them! Beyond individual obscenities, indecent language is also prohibited even if none of the typical obscenities are thrown into the mix. Transmit responsibly, even when others may not on rare occasions.

T1D06

b. **Broadcasting: FCC rules define broadcasting as the transmission of information intended for reception by the general public. Amateur stations are authorized to transmit signals related to broadcasting, program production, or news gathering only where such communication is directly related to the immediate safety of human life or protection of property and no other communication means is available.** A "CQ" or other open call indicates specifically to hams that you are listening or wish to initiate a QSO. It is *not* a general public announcement. But this regulation denies broadcasting a "regularly scheduled radio show," for instance, to anyone listening to the airwaves, whether licensed hams or shortwave receiver enthusiasts.

T1D10

T1D09

FCC exceptions to this rule do allow broadcasting for stations transmitting (Morse) **code practice** (for decoding practice), **information bulletins, or emergency communications.**

T1D12

c. **Codes or ciphers conceal or hide the meaning of messages and are prohibited from use except when transmitting control commands to space stations or radio controlled craft.** While CW Morse Code is approved, it is an open code that does not conceal meaning. You may not create your own secret code, verbal or otherwise, and transmit it on amateur radio frequencies.

T1D03

d. **Music transmissions are prohibited except when incidental to retransmission of manned spacecraft communications.** If you hear music from the International Space Station in a transmission or retransmission, that is no violation. However, if you hear Stu playing his banjo and singing on the amateur frequencies, remind him of this FCC regulation and politely encourage him to cease and desist immediately. No originals and no covers allowed.

T1D04

e. **Harmful Interference: That which seriously degrades, obstructs, or repeatedly interrupts a radio communication**

T1A04

Figure 2.1: Some FCC Prohibited Activities for Amateurs

service operating in accordance with the radio regulations. Purposeful transmission on a frequency in use or with intent to block another legal operator's transmissions falls into this category. **At no time is willful interference to other amateur radio stations permitted!** Remember, no station has sole rights to any frequency, so be polite and willing to move to another frequency if conflicting opinions arise regarding frequency use.

f.   **Retransmission** of commercial, public, or entertainment radio or television stations is prohibited. Turn down that TV or radio in the background and never purposefully retransmit a broadcast service.

g.   However, **you MAY retransmit, usually by automatic means, signals from an auxiliary, repeater, or space station** (including satellites). For instance, you may hear on a repeater a retransmission of an ISS ARISS contact: *Amateur Radio on the International*

T1A11

T1D07

Space Station. The ARISS program sponsored by the ARRL arranges amateur radio conversations between astronauts on ISS and earthly schools, museums, science centers, and community youth organizations. As a licensed Technician you may be able to arrange an ARISS contact for your school or organization!

5. **Sale or trade of equipment notifications may be transmitted as long as the equipment is normally used in an amateur radio station and this activity is not conducted regularly.** So, you cannot conduct *Bob's Radio Trade Hour* every Saturday afternoon at 1800 UTC, but you can occasionally notify others that you have some radio equipment for sale. Further, you should not be advertising your old truck for sale either – unless perhaps it comes free with the sale of a very nice mobile radio station that it happens to be wrapped around. (Just kidding – don't skirt the rules!)

6. **Payment or compensation for radio operation of a station may be received only by teachers being paid during communications incidental to classroom instruction at an educational institution.** Don't accept any money or gifts from your neighbor for making a regular radio contact with his son who is deployed to a remote island with few modern communication means. Do it simply because it is the neighborly thing to do, and be sure to reference *third party communications* in Section 2.4. However, if you are being paid as an instructor and use amateur radio communications as part of your lesson, you may receive your normal compensation for teaching.

7. **Military Station Contacts are allowed only during an Armed Forces Day Communications Test,** an annual event.

Your License: Beyond the SEVEN BIG RULES just covered, FCC Part 97 also governs issuance of amateur radio licenses and their effective terms. As noted in the *Before We Begin* section, **the FCC currently makes available three new license classes: Technician, General, and Amateur Extra** classes. Your singular license grant is issued for the combination station and operator.

Universal Licensing System (ULS): The FCC ULS contains all licensing information. It is accessible by internet and is an easily searchable database where you will find your license information.

License Effective Date: You may operate a transmitter on amateur frequencies as soon as your station/operator license grant appears in the FCC's license database. Following your successful licensing examination, your license will appear in the ULS usually within a few days. The FCC will also mail a copy of your license to the address registered on your examination forms.

T1C08 License Term: **Normally your station/operator license grant is issued for a 10 year term** that may be renewed without re-examination. No additional examination is required to renew your license as long as you do not wait too long to do it! Your license will expire after 10 years.

T1C09 T1C11 Expired Licenses: **You have a two year 'grace period' during which the license may be renewed without examination,** and after which the license and call sign are lost. **You may NOT TRANSMIT during the grace period. You must wait until the license renewal is shown on the FCC license database.**

How's it feel? Now you know some of the most important FCC rules about playing the ham radio game, so follow them to play well! But, there are still a few more things you must know before you are cut loose on your own to wield an amateur transceiver. Next we'll get at the issue of "control" of your station, and it has a specific meaning in ham radio.

But first, go whip through the exam questions for *The FCC & You*, **Section 2.1**.

www.HamRadioSchool.com/tech_media

Summary Table of the SEVEN BIG RULES:

1.	You must make your station available for FCC inspection upon request.
2.	Maintain a correct mailing address with the FCC or your license may be revoked or suspended.
3.	Use the minimum necessary power to carry out the desired communication.
4.	Prohibited Activities: - Obscene or indecent language - General broadcasting (except code - Codes or ciphers practice, bulletins, & emergencies) - Harmful/willful interference - Music transmissions (except inci- - Retransmission of commercial dental to manned spacecraft) broadcasts
5.	Sale or trade of radio gear OK if not conducted regularly.
6.	No payment or compensation except for communications incidental to classroom instruction at an educational institution.
7.	Military station contacts allowed only during Armed Forces Day Communications Tests.

Summary Table of FCC License Term Provisions

1.	The FCC currently issues three classes of new amateur licenses: Technician, General, and Amateur Extra.
2.	You may operate on the air as soon as your name and call sign appear on the FCC ULS database.
3.	Normal amateur license issued for 10 year term.
4.	Two year grace period to renew after expiration of license.
5.	No transmitting allowed during 2 year grace period until license is renewed in FCC license database.

When transmitting, an amateur station must have a control operator with license class privileges for the band and frequency of the transmission. Here Cole WØCOL is a General Class control operator overseeing the transmissions of two Technician Class licensees, Kyle KYØHIP and Quentin KDØKGJ, who are trying their hands at 20-meter HF SSB operations during Boy Scout summer camp. Cole is the responsible station control operator, and Kyle and Quentin must use Cole's call sign in station identification. Let's get into station control and make sure you have a solid understanding of these regulations...

FCC Rules & Regs

2.2   **Controlling Your Station**

" *I cannot trust a man to control others who cannot control himself. — Robert E. Lee*

Quite a few questions on THE RULES topic so far, huh? All those possible exam questions give you some indication how important it is to know and to follow THE RULES. There are a few more important regulations to know about some very practical things. For instance, who can use your radio? Can another licensed operator transmit with your station? If you're using your General licensed friend's radio, can you transmit on General class frequencies with your Technician license?

As the designated licensee for your station, you are responsible for the emissions from your radio station. Unless you have designated otherwise, you are the *control operator* for your station. **An amateur station is never permitted to transmit without a control operator.**

Control Operator: An amateur operator **designated by the licensee of an amateur station** to also be responsible for the emissions from that station. **Only a person for whom an amateur operator/primary station license grant appears in the FCC database or who is authorized for alien reciprocal operation may be designated as the control operator by the station licensee.**

The control operator may be the station licensee or another licensed operator designated by the licensee. However, the person whose name appears on the station license and FCC database, **the station licensee, is the control operator presumed by the FCC unless documentation to the contrary is in the station records.**

So, you can let your ham licensed buddy use your radio as long as he understands that he is assuming the role of control operator and is responsible for the transmissions. As the station's primary licensee, you have the power to determine who is in control of your station! **But when you give control operator responsibility to your buddy, both you (the station licensee) and he (the control operator) are equally responsible for proper operation of the station.** Be sure your buddy knows the rules, too, and that he will follow them! *Can you trust him to control himself?*

T1F10

peater Control: Practically speaking, repeaters are dumb. Really dumb. They just automatically parrot back whatever is transmitted to them. Can the repeater or repeater operator be held responsible for repeating another station's rule violation? No! **The control operator of the originating station is accountable should a repeater inadvertently retransmit communications that violate the FCC rules.**

T1E04

Frequency Privileges: Remember the question posed at the beginning of this section: If you're using your General licensed friend's radio, can you transmit on General class frequencies with your Technician license? No! **The class of operator license held by the control operator determines the transmitting privileges of an amateur station.** So if you're a Technician licensee and your friend is a General or Amateur Extra licensee, you may use his station as control operator only on Technician frequencies. But...

www.scouting.org/jota
Photo: James, KDØMFO

Figure 2.2: Third Party Communicator and Control Operator

A control operator may allow an unlicensed person (third party) to transmit on amateur bands, but the radio is still under control of the licensee whose FCC call sign is used to identify the station. Hams and Boy Scouts convene annually for Jamboree on the Air (JOTA), providing scouts a taste of ham radio excitement, including international contacts, by third party communication. Here Eric, KDØMUW, helps Garrett make his first ham radio contact on a local repeater.

If your General licensed friend remains the control operator, present at the radio station's *control point* with you, you can transmit on General class frequencies under his supervision and using his station call sign. This is a fine point, but remember it depends on who is the designated control operator. **Under normal circumstances, a station operating in the exclusive General or Extra Class operator segment of an amateur band may never have a Technician class licensee control operator.** Similarly, a General licensee may never be control operator for a station operating in the exclusive Extra class portion of a band. It's all about the control operator's license.

Control Point: Note that your General class buddy has to be with you at the radio's **control point – that's the location at which the control operator function is performed.** For most stations the control point is going to be in front of the radio where the knobs and dials are located. Or with an HT, the control point is in the palm of your hand. 'Duh!' right?

Local Control: The control operator is at the station control point and can immediately manipulate the station operating adjustments. Handheld radios are almost always locally controlled.

Well, it's not always quite that simple because ham radio operators are clever and innovative types! Ham radios, such as some repeaters, can be operated from a distance through radio frequency controls, such as with an *auxiliary station*. Others may be connected to the internet via a computer and operated from that wi-fi hot spot down at the coffee shop using a laptop. And then there are those automatic repeaters on a frozen mountain top with nobody around for miles. What then?

Remote Control: When the control operator is not at the station location but can indirectly manipulate the operating adjustments of the station, remote control is being used. This includes the radio link-controlled scenario. A common **example of remote control is operating the station over the Internet.** But all the control operator rules still apply, even if you're not physically in front of your radio.

Automatic Control: The control operator is not present at a control point. Automatic Control is the only type of control in which it is permissible for the control operator to be at a location other than a control point. **Repeater operation is an example of automatic control.**

So, careful leaving your HT or car mobile station unattended where some self-proclaimed jokester can help you violate FCC regs! People are curious, after all. Explain the FCC rules and let them try it under your control, and help them become a licensed ham, too!

T1E12

T1E05

T1E09

T1E10

T1E08

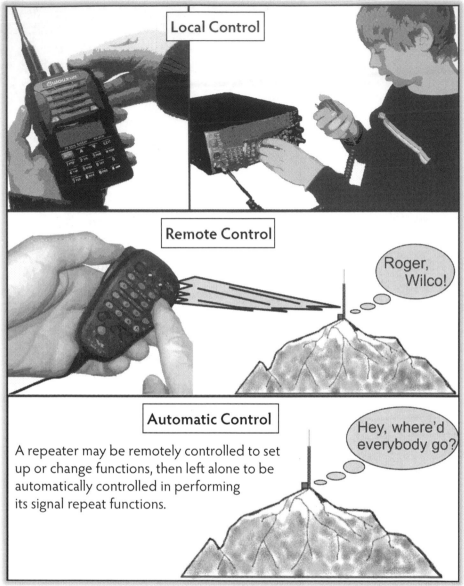

Figure 2.3 Three Types of Station Control

I hope that now you can control yourself! Or at least control your radio station properly. Always make sure there is a control operator for all your station's transmissions, and make sure those transmissions are legal for the control operator's license class. It's about that simple.

Let's hit the **Section 2.2** question pool! Last one in is QRN! ☺
www.HamRadioSchool.com/tech_media

FCC Rules & Regs

2.3
Call Signs

> **" We all have such common ways to identify with each other... it's almost indescribable how it connects human to human... — Debby Boone**

Intertwined with the topic of control is the matter of identifying on the air, and hams have a common way of doing this with call signs. But with all respect to Debby, it's really not that difficult to describe how call signs connect us.

In most cases you'll be using your FCC-assigned call sign without modification to identify your station. But there are some special circumstances where you might need to make a slight modification or use another type of call sign altogether. And of course, you need to be familiar with FCC regulations governing call sign formats and use.

Call Sign: A unique alphanumeric identifier assigned by the FCC to a licensed operator-station pairing. No one else has your call sign – it identifies you and your station only. In the amateur service your license is granted for the pairing of operator and station, and your call sign points to both. Your call sign is you. Use it loudly and proudly!

Identification on the Air: We've covered this already, but it bears repeating: **An amateur station is required to transmit its assigned call sign at least every 10 minutes during, and at the end of, a contact.**

T1F03

Use English or CW: The English language is the only acceptable language for use for station identification when operating in a phone (voice) sub-band. You may also use CW (Morse Code characters) to identify when transmitting phone signals, but this is uncommon except for repeater stations. Although, if you really want to whistle or toot out a little CW tone sequence instead of easily stating a few letters and numbers, you are in compliance doing so. Other hams will just think you're a little weird!

T1F04 T1F05

Phonetics: Papa, **H**otel, **O**scar, **N**ovember, **E**cho, **T**ango, **I**ndia, **C**harlie, **S**ierra! Those are standard phonetic alphabet characters. They come in handy in

A – Alpha	J – Juliet	S – Sierra
B – Bravo	K – Kilo	T – Tango
C – Charlie	L – Lima	U – Uniform
D – Delta	M – Mike	V – Victor
E – Echo	N – November	W – Whiskey
F – Foxtrot	O – Oscar	X – X-Ray
G – Golf	P – Papa	Y – Yankee
H – Hotel	Q – Quebec	Z – Zulu
I – India	R – Romeo	

The International Telecommunications Union Standard Phonetic Alphabet

Figure 2.4: ITU Standard Phonetics

T2C03

noisy and weak signal conditions to help positively exchange call signs. **To insure voice messages containing proper names and unusual words are copied correctly by receiving stations, such words and terms should be spelled out using a standard phonetic alphabet.** Although they are less frequently used on FM repeaters or simplex communications, phonetics are almost always used in the noisier HF SSB conditions. **The FCC**

T2B09

encourages the use of a phonetic alphabet when identifying your station using phone modes.

Call Sign Formats: Call signs are formatted with sequences of letters and numbers. In the US, standard amateur radio station call signs must begin with A, K, N, or W, and they must have a single digit number that is preceded by one or two letters (the prefix) and followed by one to three letters (the suffix). In some special circumstances some additional self-assigned characters may be added after the suffix.

The following are the valid US standard amateur call sign formats. In the format templates below, the X's are alphabet letter places, and the Ø is the number placeholder for any digit 0 to 9.

> **2x3 Format:** XXØXXX   Examples: KF5CLZ, KTØLIZ
> May be held by any license class.
> Must begin with KA – KZ or WA – WZ.

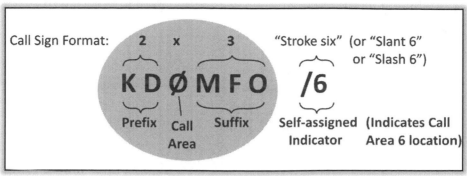

Figure 2.5: Dissection of a US Call Sign

New Technicians are usually assigned 2x3 format call signs by the FCC from an alphabetical sequence. This will be you!

1x3 Format: XØXXX **Example: W3ABC**
May be held by Technician, General, Advanced, or Extra class licensees. Must begin with K, N, or W.

2x2 Format: XXØXX Examples: KBØSA, WR1GL
May be held by Advanced or Extra class licensees.
Must begin with KA – KZ, NA – NZ, or WA – WZ for Advanced class.
May also begin with AA – AK for Extra class.

1x2 and 2x1 Formats: XØXX and XXØX Examples: KØNR and AAØK
May be held only by Extra class licensees.
May begin with K, N, W, or AA – AK (with some specific exclusions)

1x1 Format: XØX Example: W8M
Special Event Call Sign format, has a single letter in both prefix and suffix. It is temporarily issued for stations operating in conjunction with an activity of special significance to the amateur community. Effective term is usually not more than a few days.

Notice that for the zero digit in several of the example call signs here a 'slash zero' (Ø) character is used. This helps to easily differentiate zero from the letter 'O' and is common practice among the ham community.

Vanity Call Signs: A vanity call sign is a valid call sign for the license class specified by the amateur licensee. **Under the vanity call sign rules any licensed amateur may select a desired call sign** (subject to availability). **For example, K1XXX is a vanity call sign that a Technician Class operator might select if it is available,** not already assigned to another licensee. This vanity call sign could replace a 2x3 format call sign initially issued by the FCC to a new Technician Class licensee.

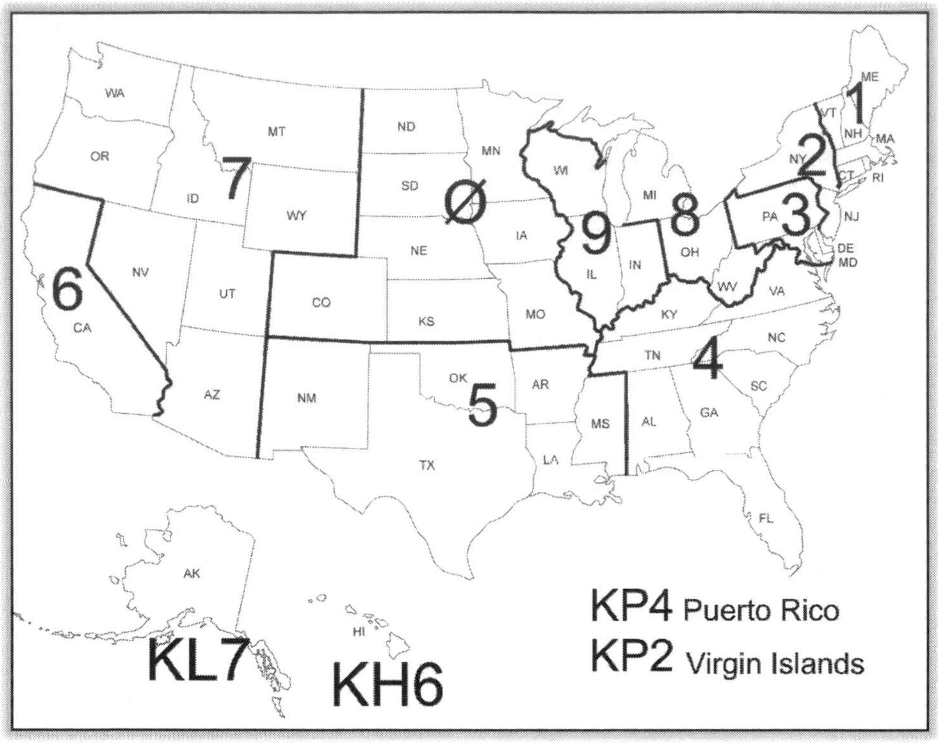

Figure 2.6: US Amateur Radio Call Districts

Call Areas or Districts: In the United States the single digit of the call sign separating the prefix and suffix indicates the geographic call area in which the license was awarded. These are also known as call *districts*. After a call sign is issued the call area number within it does not change even if the licensee permanently relocates to another call area, unless the licensee requests a new call sign be issued. As a result, call district indicators do not always match the registered transmitting location of a station.

Club Call Signs: The FCC will issue a unique call sign for organizations with a primary purpose of amateur radio service and with a **membership of at least 4 persons.** Club license grants must have **a designated trustee** who is responsible for the use of the call sign by the organization and **who may select a vanity call sign for the club,** if desired. The frequency privileges of a club call sign are determined by the privileges of the trustee, but all control operator regulations must still be followed when transmitting using a club call sign. So, as a Technician you cannot use your Extra class club's call sign to jump on the Extra class exclusive frequencies as a control operator! Nice try though.

T1F12

T1C14

Tactical Call Signs: *"Roger Headquarters! Team Mole Rat has located the fox!"* These are **tactical call signs,** "Headquarters" and "Team Mole Rat." Tactical call signs typically describe a position, a responsibility, or an affiliation with an easy-to-understand name. "Parade Start, Announcer's Booth, or **Race Headquarters**" are additional examples. You and your group of hams can **use tactical identifiers, but you must still comply with the 10-minute and end-of-communication identification rules with your FCC assigned call sign.** So: *"Team Mole Rat is clearing off the frequency for lunch. WØSTU."*

Self-Assigned Call Sign Indicators: You can add some indicators to the end of your call sign to help avoid confusion and make clear your transmitting situation. For example, if you take your radio to another numbered call district and operate from there, you should make it known that you are operating from outside of your normal station call district by adding a self-assigned indicator. See the examples below.

There are **three different formats for stating a self-assigned call sign indicator on the air.** Take your pick. You can say:

"KL7CC **stroke** W3," "KL7CC **slant** W3," or "KL7CC **slash** W3"

They all mean the same thing, that KL7CC is visiting somewhere East, and not home in Homer, Alaska as usual. (The "W" is a standard used to indicate a US call area in the lower 48 states, in this example's case US call area 3.)

Similarly, **when a new license privilege has been earned by CSCE, the FCC requires the operator to add indicators for the new license class until the upgraded license appears in the FCC license database: /KT, /AG, or /AE for upgraded Technician, General, or Extra.**

"Dung Beetle to Book Reader – you've completed another section! Way to go! See how this tactical call sign connects us? Over."

You can have fun with your call sign, with a tactical call sign, or even just with the way you *say it with flare on the air!* I always enjoy adding just a little extra punch to my call sign, especially on days off work. Rattling off your new call sign will quickly become as easy and flowing as a slick nickname in no time.

"Book Reader – Now try the question pool items for **Section 2.3!** 73. WØSTU, clear."

www.HamRadioSchool.com/tech_media

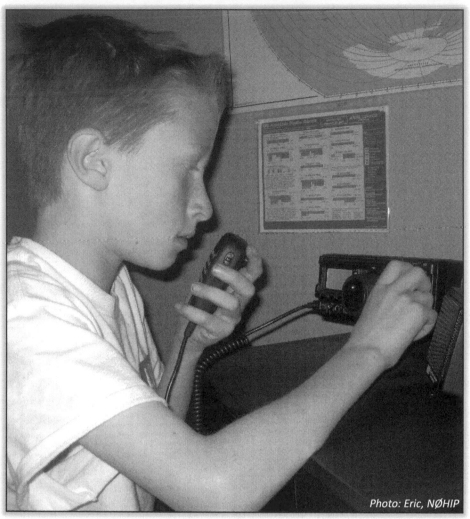

Photo: Eric, NØHIP

Ten is a lucky number for Brandon, KDØPWF. He earned his Technician license at 10 years old and immediately began working 10 meters. He quickly qualified for *10-10 International Net* membership, and within four months of licensing he had earned the *Worked All Continents* award, making radio contact with operators from every continent on earth. With his 10-meter Technician privileges, Brandon is really *talking to the world!*

Learn more about 10-10 International: www.ten-ten.org

❝ *It was impossible to get a conversation going, everybody was talking too much. — Yogi Berra*

So you're howling your call sign comfortably, sticking to all the rules, and feeling good! Then you run out and purchase a SSB radio so you can reach out on the 10 meter band Technician frequencies and make contacts around the globe. Wow! That will be exciting, *talking to everyone so much!*

But, what are the rules for reaching out beyond the US national borders? Are there countries that are banned from amateur communications? Can you get into trouble literally *talking too much internationally?* What if you're interfering with stations outside the US? What if you're on a ship in international waters? Hrmmm…. Some more things to know about the rules, yes. Let's take a look at talking to the world.

Radio communications that can traverse the planet require a little coordination among nations. Otherwise we would all be interfering with one another and not making efficient use of the available radio spectrum. To help get things coordinated a **United Nations agency for information and communication technology issues has been established: The International Telecommunications Union, or ITU.** T1B01

ITU Regions: The ITU separates the world into three geographic regions for assigning and coordinating radio frequency use. These regions are depicted in Figure 2.7 on the following page. North American amateur stations are in ITU Region 2. **Some US territories are located in ITU regions other than region 2, and frequency assignments are different from the 50 US states.** An FCC-licensed station must abide by the frequencies assigned to the ITU region from which it operates. T1B02

International Waters: Within the international agreements made through the ITU, the FCC governs all spectrum use and radio stations inside the US, and **FCC licensed amateur stations may transmit from any vessel or craft located in international waters that is documented or registered in the United States.** So, as long as your US-registered yacht is out on the high seas outside of the international boundary of another nation, you can PTT with liberty and confidence under your FCC license. T1C06

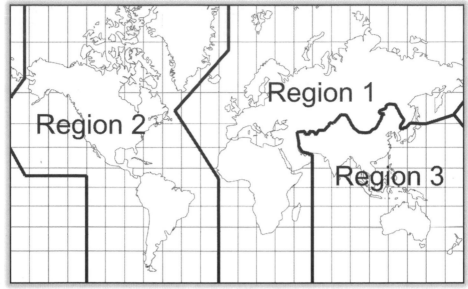

Figure 2.7: ITU Regions

However, **the frequency assignments for US stations operating maritime mobile will not be the same everywhere in the world since the amateur frequency assignments vary among the three ITU regions.** Be mindful of these variations if you operate on the high seas!

Foreign Contacts and Communications: **One purpose of the Amateur Radio Service as defined by FCC rules is that of enhancing international goodwill.** But, foreign contacts and communications are limited by some nations and by agreements (or lack thereof) between nations. **FCC** **licensed stations are permitted to make international communications that are incidental to the purposes of the amateur service and remarks of a personal character.** What's that mean? Normal chit-chat about life and work, discussions about radio, call sign exchanges of course. It is prudent to minimize political conversations in some nations. However, **FCC** **licensed stations are prohibited from exchanging communications with any country whose administration has notified the ITU that it objects to such communications.** You will not likely hear from North Korea, for instance.

Third Party Communications: FCC Part 97.3 defines the term "third-party communication" as a message from the control operator (first party) of an amateur station to another amateur station control operator (second party) on behalf of another person (third party). Third party communication is also construed sometimes to be a non-licensed person transmitting on your radio under your licensed control operator supervision. Some countries get a little antsy about this sort of thing.

Third party communications of a non-emergency nature are authorized by the FCC with any foreign station whose government permits such communications. Check the international agreements before you allow international third party communications with your station! **The foreign station must be one with which the US has a third party agreement when a Technician Class control operator allows a non-licensed person to speak to the foreign station.** Completely within the US, have no worries about third parties. It's done all the time.

International Interference: We will discuss some technical methods for elimination of interference in Chapter 12, but your responsibility to eliminate interference extends even to foreign stations. **On any band, if you learn that you are interfering with** another radio station or another radio service altogether (commercial stations, **radiolocation stations,** military, etc.) **outside of the US, you must stop operating or take steps to eliminate the harmful interference.**

Radionavigation Service is protected from interference by amateur signals under all circumstances. As a Technician Class licensee with privileges in the 70-centimeter band (see Section 4.2), be aware that **the amateur service is secondary in some portions of the 70 cm band, so US amateurs may find non-amateur stations in the band and must avoid interfering with them.** (This is not a common scenario within the contiguous US states.)

Operating in Foreign Countries: There are many reasons you may want to transmit from another country. Many hams enjoy the challenge and thrill of "*DXpeditions*," where operators travel to activate stations in foreign and possibly hard-to-contact geographical areas to help make DX radio contacts (distant contacts outside the US). However, **you may operate your amateur station in a foreign country only when authorized by that country.** Check the law of foreign nations well before traveling and transmitting! Many nations have *reciprocal agreements* with the US, allowing amateur stations to freely operate in each agreed nation with little or no red tape.

Standing International Agreements: The United States participates in a couple of international organizations in which reciprocal amateur radio communications licensing is recognized. However, be aware that the licensing requirements among participating nations do not align perfectly, so the reciprocity agreements are not applicable to all US license classes.

Photo: Steve, WGØAT

Figure 2.8: Ham Radio Hardship — Caribbean Island DXpedition!

CEPT: European Conference of Postal and Telecommunications Administrations (CEPT acronym is a French interpretation). CEPT is an organization of European nations and participating countries outside of Europe that share amateur radio licensing reciprocal requirements. Currently this reciprocity applies for FCC General class licenses and above, and there is no reciprocity agreement currently for FCC Technicians.

IARP: International Amateur Radio Permit. This permit may be issued to amateurs wishing to operate in member nations of *The Inter-American Telecommunications Commission* (CITEL). Many North and South American countries accept IARP, including: Argentina, Brazil, Canada, El Salvador, Panama, Peru, Trinidad and Tobago, United States of America, Uruguay, and Venezuela. There are two classes of IARPs, each with restrictions. Class 1 requires knowledge of international Morse Code, but carries all operating privileges. Class 2 does not require Morse Code, but is limited to 30 MHz and higher frequencies (10m – 70cm bands and higher).

Most exchanges with foreign countries on the HF bands will probably be brief exchanges of call signs and perhaps light greetings and pleasantries. It's not that easy to get into trouble on the air, so don't fret. Still, make sure you understand your responsibilities according to the regulations and our international agreements. Your international contacts will be much more enjoyable and rewarding that way. *Capice?*

Konnichiwa! You have completed another advancement of your ham radio knowledge! Get online and try the **Section 2.4** questions for this section now, *hi hi.*

www.HamRadioSchool.com/tech_media

Buddipole's Chris, W6HFP, sets up a Mini-Buddipole on the east coast of 8P6/Barbados. Operations from foreign countries can be both rewarding and challenging! Photo by Steve, WG0AT; Courtesy Buddipole www.buddipole.com

Figure 3.0: James KDØMFO blends his hobbies of backpacking and amateur radio by competing in a VHF contest from a mountaintop location using a battery powered portable station. The contest goal is to make as many contacts a possible across as many geographic grid locations as possible within the contest's duration. You can contest from the comfort of your home shack or even from your car's mobile station, leaving the mountain climbing for another day! Contesting is just one of many intriguing *Things To Do* with amateur radio!

3.0 Things to Do!

" *Amateur Radio: The first technology-based social network. — Anonymous*

So, what kinds of things do ham radio operators do besides just jaw and be social? What kind of fun things and what kind of important things can you get involved with once you have your license? Are there contests? How can you be prepared to help with communications in an emergency?

Amateur Radio offers an incredible breadth of rewarding activities. Whether you are interested in amateur radio as a technical hobby, as an effective learning tool, for emergency preparedness, for community service, or for other reasons all your own, you are sure to find many of the facets of amateur radio intriguing, challenging, and addicting! The following descriptions barely scratch the surface of all the things you can do with ham radio, but these are some of the most common activities, and the ones for which exam questions are waiting!

Nets: A radio net is an on-air meeting of a group of amateur operators. Often a radio club or group with common interests will hold regularly scheduled nets. Repeaters or simplex frequencies may be used to convene a net. Nets usually have a designated net control station that is responsible for keeping the flow of transmissions from participants orderly, sequencing discussion topics like a meeting leader, and requesting responses station-by-station to avoid "doubles" where more than one station transmits simultaneously. Participating in an open net is a great way to get started practicing your new skills on the air with other friendly ham operators!

Traffic: With its roots deep in the message relaying historical service of amateur radio, *traffic* is a message to be disseminated or relayed. The term traffic is commonly used now to refer more generally to any information relevant to the net. Often near the beginning of a net and commonly combined with your check in transmission of your call sign and name, you will be asked to indicate whether or not you have traffic for the net. If you have an announcement that is of general interest to the group you should check in to the net "*with traffic*" and await recognition by net control to make your comments.

Priority or Emergency Traffic: An accepted practice during net operations to get the immediate attention of the net control station when reporting an emergency is to begin your transmission by saying "Priority" or "Emergency" followed by your call sign. Although rarely implemented, this procedure is recognized universally as a means of getting quick response in handling an emergency, since a net is a structured conversation of multiple transmissions that may consume a significant amount of air time and make it otherwise difficult to break in.

Message Traffic Handling: One of the original and valuable services provided by amateur radio operators that is still used today is message traffic handling. Message traffic handling is particularly valuable during natural disasters when other means of communication are not operable. Formal message traffic handling uses a very specific format to help ensure the accuracy of relayed messages is preserved across multiple relay radio stations. *Radiograms* may be addressed to anyone in the general public or to another licensed amateur radio operator. The radiogram is transmitted from station to station cross-

Number	Precedence	HX	Station of Origin	Check	Place of Origin	Time Filed	Date

Amateur Radio Message Radiogram

To:

This radio message was received at:
Station_____ Date _____
Name _____
Street Address _____
City, State, Zip _____

Telephone Number:

Received: From Date Time   Sent: To Date Time

Figure 3.1: A Typical Message Traffic Handling Radiogram Form

country until the designated addressee is contacted. A couple of radiogram parts bear noting:

Preamble: **The preamble of a formal traffic message is the information needed to track the message as it passes through the amateur radio traffic handling system.** A preamble usually contains a message identification number, a message priority, the originating station, the date, and the place of origin, and a *check number.* Other optional handling instructions may also be provided.

[T2C10]

Check: **The check** in reference to a formal traffic message **is a count of the number of words or word equivalents in the text portion of the message.** Radiogram messages are usually brief messages not longer than 25 words. The check helps ensure that the relayed message has been accurately received by a station for retransmission. The radiogram form of Figure 3.1 has spaces for five words per line to make word counting easy.

[T2C11]

Contesting is a popular operating activity that involves contacting as many stations as possible during a specified period of time. Contests may specify the bands and modes allowed for contest contacts, as well as other rules. Contests are a great way to gauge the transmissions of your station for distance and quality.

[T8C03]

Contest Contacts: **A good procedure when contacting another station in a radio contest is to send only the minimum information needed for proper identification and the contest exchange.** Check the contest rules for required information exchange before making contacts. Frequently the required exchange will include your geographic location, usually in terms of the Maidenhead Grid Square locator system. This minimum information transmission is a good policy since contesters are trying to make as many contacts as possible in a limited time and do not wish to "*rag chew*" (have an extended casual conversation).

[T8C04]

Grid Locator: **A grid locator, or Maidenhead Grid Locator, is a letter-number designator assigned to a geographic location.** The basic grid square unit designated by a four character designator (two letters followed by two numbers) is a 1 x 2 degree area on the earth's surface. (See Figure 3.2.)

[T8C05]

Hidden Transmitter Hunt are also known as "*foxhunts.*" **A directional antenna** or similar equipment **is used to locate a hidden transmitter** in this challenging and competitive activity. Foxhunts take many different forms and may require navigation by automobile, by foot, or by other means. Amateur radio clubs often sponsor foxhunts. You can get started in foxhunting with

[T8C02]

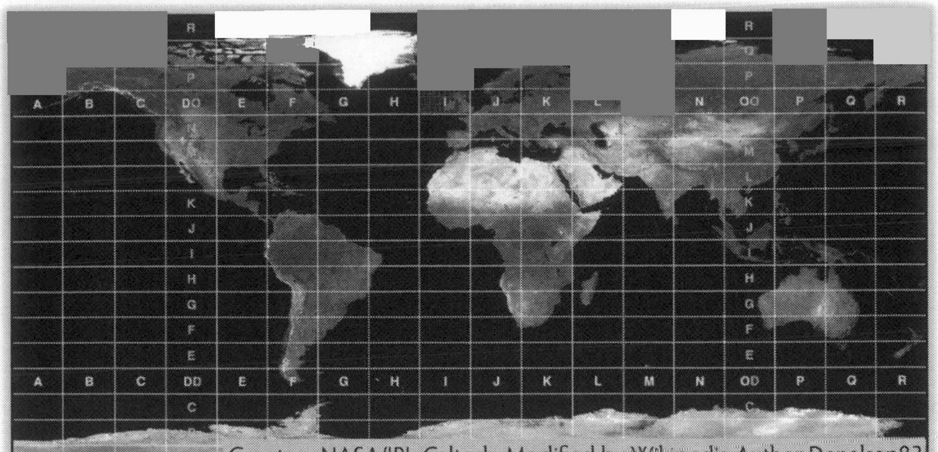

Courtesy NASA/JPL-Caltech; Modified by Wikipedia Author Denelson83

The Maidenhead grid locator system is frequently used to exchange geographic locations in radio contests. Two letters identify longitude-latitude grids by the matrix depicted above, and each grid is subdivided into smaller "squares" of 1x2 degrees, each designated by a pair of numbers following the grid letters. The author resides within DM79.

Figure 3.2: Maidenhead Grid Square Locator System

simple and inexpensive homemade or kit-built equipment combined with a common VHF or UHF HT radio.

Emergency Services: Amateur radio operators may provide emergency communication services in concert with public officials and organizations. **Two organizations having the common purpose of providing communications during emergencies are RACES and ARES.** In many areas RACES and ARES organizations will hold regular nets for the coordination of their volunteers, training, and equipment.

> **RACES: Radio Amateur Civil Emergency Service uses amateur frequencies and stations for emergency management or civil defense communications.** RACES defines a protocol created by the FCC and by the Federal Emergency Management Agency (FEMA) for training and deploying volunteer radio operators in times of civil emergency. **RACES amateur operators are certified and enrolled by a civil defense organization** and may be activated by local, county, or state jurisdictions to assist with drills, exercises, and emergencies.

> **ARES: Amateur Radio Emergency Service consists of licensed amateurs who have voluntarily registered their qualifications and equipment with local ARES leadership for communications**

T2C04

T2C05

T2C12

duty in the public service. Local level organizations determine the training requirements to participate fully in local ARES organizations.

Special Rules for Emergencies: When normal communications systems are not available **in situations involving the immediate safety of human life or the protection of property, amateur station control operators may operate outside the frequency privileges of their license class** and use any means of radio communication for essential communications. However, when using amateur radio simply at the request of public service officials, normal FCC rules still apply. The danger to human life or to property is the determining factor for deviating from any of the FCC rules.

Emergency Nets: In emergencies special radio nets may be established for the handling of emergency traffic. **Once you have checked in to an emergency traffic net, remain on frequency without transmitting until asked to do so by the net control station** in order to minimize disruptions to emergency traffic. **An important characteristic of good emergency traffic handling is passing messages exactly as received!** Use phonetics to spell out names or difficult terms and insure precise and accurate communications.

Photos: ©2010 Beth Wald

Boy Scouts of Colorado Troop 6 compete in GeoFox around a mountain course. Finding a geocache using a GPS receiver gives a frequency for a hidden transmitter to be hunted with a directional antenna. The fox reveals the next geocache coordinate. Scout teams compete for best time completing a challenging course mixing foxhunting & geocaching.

Figure 3.3: Hidden Transmitter 'Foxhunt' with a GeoTwist

Now you understand just a few of the fun and important kinds of activities you can be involved with in amateur radio. Whether serving as a RACES or ARES emergency communications volunteer during a hurricane or wildfire evacuation, passing vital message traffic following an earthquake or tsunami, or helping local authorities manage communications outside the perimeter of a railway chemical spill, YOU can make a difference and serve your community. And after the emergency is passed you can tell your exciting emergency war story on the weekly net, enjoy a foxhunt, activate a SOTA peak (see Figures 3.5 and 3.6), or see how many contacts you can make in a radio contest! As a ham radio operator you can work hard, play hard, and love it all!

Go tackle the exam questions for **Section 3.0** at *HamRadioSchool.com* and think about all the things you'd like to do as a licensed amateur!

www.HamRadioSchool.com/tech_media

Photo: Bob, NØTDX

Figure 3.4: Colorado 14er Radio Event: Mountain Top Contacts!
Each August hams summit 14,000'+ mountains all across Colorado to make VHF and UHF simplex contacts. You can get incredible range from peak-to-peak! Here Randy, KNØTPC, and Andrew, KDØLLC, work 2m and 6m from Pikes Peak. Some peaks get activated with HF rigs as well and make worldwide contacts.

Figure 3.5 & 3.6: Summits On the Air (SOTA)

Steve, WGØAT, is frequently enlisted as control operator for goats Peanut, Barley, and Acorn who enjoy SOTA action. *www.youtube.com/goathiker*

SOTA is an award program for radio amateurs encouraging portable operation in mountainous areas. You don't have to climb even a small hill to participate!

Photos: Steve, WGØAT

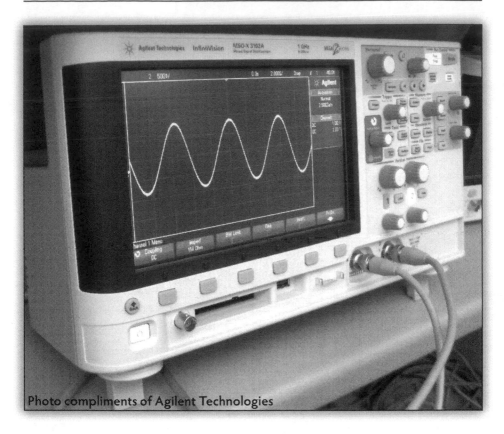

Photo compliments of Agilent Technologies

Figure 4.0: An oscilloscope is an electronic measurement instrument that can display an input voltage signal over time, allowing us to see waveforms in the time domain. It paints a dynamic picture of an AC waveform's voltage variations. The scope operator may change the range of time displayed across the horizontal extent of the screen to "zoom in or out" to inspect the waveform. The vertical voltage scale may also be adjusted to aid viewing. Oscilloscopes are very useful for evaluating the quality and characteristics of RF signals, including frequency, wavelength, and waveform consistency. They are often used to evaluate and troubleshoot transmitters and receivers. Let's learn more about these signals that the oscilloscope helps us visualize...

4.0 Wavelength, Frequency, & Bands

" *Can ye fathom the ocean, dark and deep, where the mighty waves and the grandeur sweep? – Fanny Crosby*

Aye, aye, Mate! This chapter is an introduction to the science of radio frequency emissions and the definitions of the amateur radio bands. When you have completed Section 4.1 you will have a solid introduction to radio wave characteristics. Section 4.2 describes how we use those characteristics in the identification of the frequency bands that are allocated by the FCC for amateur radio use. Let's start with a day at the beach *fathoming the ocean, dark and deep!* (There may be sharks.)

4.1 Wavelength, Frequency, & Bands
Wavelength and Frequency

Think about the ocean. Imagine yourself on the beach if you like, with the ocean waves rolling slowly in and crashing on the shoreline. Look out, that crab is about to pinch your toe!

Wavelength: Those ocean waves have a lot in common with radio waves. They have a characteristic *wavelength,* for instance. If you were bobbing out in the water you could get an estimate of the wavelength when you are carried up to the top of a wave and are able to see straight across to the crest of the next wave coming at you. That straight line distance crest-to-crest, top-to-top of two consecutive waves, from you to that shark fin, is the wavelength. The ocean wavelength may be 50 feet, for instance. That's a long wavelength by water wave standards, but not so huge for some radio frequency waves.

You could also measure the same way between the troughs, or bottoms of the swells, and you'd get the same distance. Or you could choose to measure from

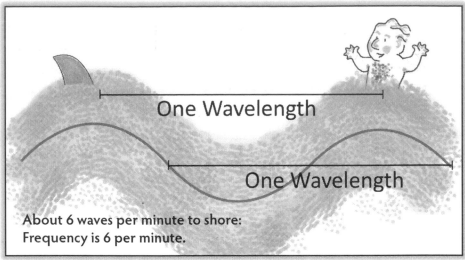

Figure 4.1: Long Wavelength and Low Frequency

exactly half way up each wave from the troughs and you would get the same measure of wavelength for regular repeating waves.

Now, you evade sharks, swim to shore, and walk over to a small tidal pool that is temporarily isolated from the great ocean waves. Only harmless minnows inhabit the little pool, *bright and shallow*. And an occasional crab, hungry for toes. Its surface is calm and still until you drop a pebble into the center of it. Miniature versions of those ocean waves ripple to the edges of the pool and you quickly estimate the distance between ripple crests to be about one inch. Those are quite short wavelengths as compared to the mighty ocean waves.

Frequency: How *frequently* do the waves come in? Looking back at the ocean waves you time their arrivals and find that about six waves roll into shore each minute. But with a pebble in the pool about 3 ripples reach the edge every second, so that would amount to 180 every minute if you continuously plopped pebbles into the water.

Those rates of wave arrival, or *frequencies* of the waves, are quite different: 6 per minute versus 180 per minute. The pool ripples arrive with higher frequency than do the ocean waves. The ocean waves are of lower frequency than the ripples. Now let's apply these characteristics of wavelength and frequency to our radio transmissions.

Electromagnetic Waves: EM waves carry radio signals between transmitting and receiving stations. EM waves oscillate like the water waves, having a characteristic wavelength and frequency. But unlike the water waves, EM waves do not require any medium like water to flow within. Rather, EM

T3A07

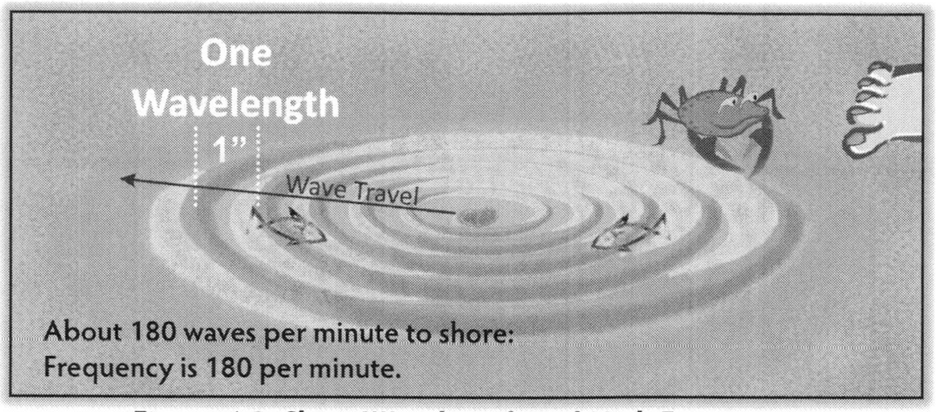

Figure 4.2: Short Wavelength and High Frequency

waves are oscillations of electric fields and magnetic fields that reinforce one another and sort of provide their own self-contained medium! **EM waves that travel through free space** – the vacuum of outer space or earth's atmosphere – **are radio waves.** T5C07

Light waves that we perceive with our eyes are one kind of EM wave. Radio waves are also EM waves, only of a much longer wavelength and lower frequency than light. Your doctor's X-rays are yet another, shorter wavelength and higher frequency EM wave.

Radio Waves: As EM waves, radio waves have the two components, the electric and magnetic fields. Like all EM waves in free space, **radio waves travel at the speed of light,** or an **approximate velocity of 300,000,000 meters per second** (300 million meters per second). This velocity does not change significantly in air or in vacuum. Good thing the ocean waves don't go that fast, huh? T3B03 T3B04 T3B11

Radio Frequency: Rather than measuring waves per minute like in the ocean and pool, radio frequencies are measured in waves (or cycles) per second, and this **unit of frequency is called hertz.** T5C05

Electromagnetic waves in the range of **radio frequency signals of all types are commonly referred to as RF,** meaning simply *radio frequencies.* RF transmissions that radiate from an antenna are originated in a transmitter with electrical currents that reverse direction in an electric circuit many times per second (alternating current, or AC). The number of AC reversals per second will generate an identical frequency RF signal from the energized antenna. **So, frequency is also used to describe the number of times that an alternating current reverses direction** in an electric circuit. T5C06 T5A12

Radio Wavelengths: Just like the ocean and pool waves, radio waves will have a characteristic wavelength that is measured between equivalent wave positions of the electric or magnetic field oscillations – crest-to-crest, for instance. Because the waves are moving through space it is easy to consider that **the distance a radio wave travels in the completion of one cycle** (one complete wave oscillation) **is its wavelength.**

Radio wavelengths are typically expressed in the unit of meters. Described this way, **the approximate wavelength of radio waves is often used to identify the different frequency bands.**

So, you will hear hams discussing the "*2 meter band*" or the "*6 meter band*" or the "*10 meter band*." This does not mean that all of the wavelengths transmitted in the 2 meter band are exactly two meters long, but rather they are *approximately* two meters in wavelength. In fact, the 2 meter band's wavelengths vary from longest to shortest over a span of about 5.5 centimeters, or about 2.25 inches, but all pretty close to two meters.

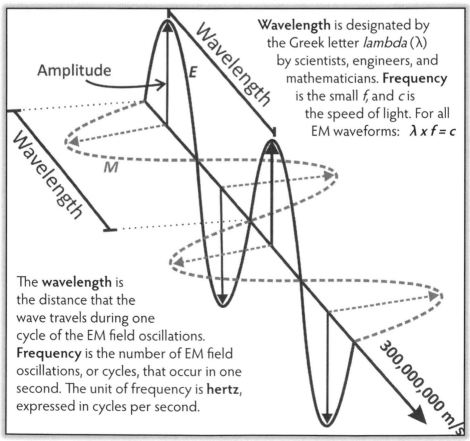

Figure 4.3: Electromagnetic Wave Wavelength and Amplitude

Wavelength-Frequency Relationship: Because radio signals travel at a constant speed, a special relationship arises between wavelength and frequency of waves. **As the wavelength gets shorter, the frequency gets higher, or increases** in hertz. Conversely, as the wavelength gets longer, the frequency gets lower, or decreases in hertz.

T3B05

Think back to the water waves: Those giant ocean waves had long wavelengths and low frequency, rolling into shore only a few times each minute. The pool ripples had short wavelengths and arrived with high frequency of well over a hundred times each minute. Radio waves work in a similar way: *long and low, short and high.*

A simple mathematical **formula** relates wavelength and frequency for all radio waves, and it is **used for converting frequency to wavelength in meters.** It is also used the other way, converting wavelength to frequency. The following equations are always true for radio signals:

T3B06

Wavelength (in meters) = 300 ÷ frequency (in megahertz)
Frequency (in megahertz) = 300 ÷ wavelength (in meters)

To use this simple relationship, the wavelength must always be expressed in meters and the frequency in millions of hertz, or "megahertz." The prefix mega means one million.

Examples: Suppose you want to know the specific wavelength for a frequency in the 2 meter band that is displayed on your radio: 146.52 MHz, the national calling frequency. Since the frequency is already provided in megahertz (MHz), it is really easy to calculate the wavelength:

Wavelength (in meters) = 300 ÷ 146.52 MHz
So, Wavelength = 2.0475 meters

You can see that this is pretty close to two meters, hence **146.52 MHz is in the "2 meter band."**

T1B04

What if you wished to determine the frequency of a wavelength 21.0 meters long? No sweat:

Frequency (in MHz) = 300 ÷ 21.0 m
Frequency = 14.286 MHz

And yes, that frequency is squarely in the "*20 meter band*" in the HF range. We'll explore more about all those bands in the next section.

Math Prefixes and Conversions: Sometimes for convenience frequencies will be expressed in other multiples of hertz besides mega, or one million. Some other common mathematical prefixes include:

kilo = 1000   as in...   kilohertz (kHz) = 1000 Hertz
Giga = 1 Billion   as in...   Gigahertz (GHz) = 1,000,000,000 Hertz

You can convert between these prefixes by moving the decimal point left or right three places for each step: Hz, kHz, MHz, GHz. To convert from a lower prefix to higher prefix, such as kilohertz to Megahertz, move the decimal left three positions (adding left zeros if needed). To convert from higher prefix to lower, such as Gigahertz to Megahertz, move the decimal right three places. To convert between greater prefix differences, such as from Gigahertz down to kilohertz, you'll have to make more than one of these step conversions -- GHz to kHz requires two decimal-moving steps, or a total of six digit positions. Let's try some examples!

Examples:

Converting high to low (GHz to MHz to kHz to Hz)
0.0015 GHz = 1.5 MHz = 1,500 kHz = 1,500,000 Hz
(Move the decimal 3 places right for each prefix step.)

Converting low to high (Hz to kHz to MHz to GHz)
3,525,000 Hz = 3,525 kHz = 3.525 MHz = 0.003525 GHz
(Move the decimal 3 places left for each prefix step.)

I like to remember this with a goofy little rhyme that refers to the prefix as either being large & hefty (like MHz or GHz), or small and slight (like kHz or Hz):

From hefty to slight, dot moves right.
From slight to hefty, dot's a lefty.

Use the examples above to see how that goofism works! The first example is hefty to slight prefixes. The second example is slight to hefty prefixes. Try a couple more from the question pool:

Covert **28,400 kHz** to megahertz (MHz). *Hint: slight to hefty, one step!*
Move the decimal left three places: **28,400 kHz = 28.400 MHz.**

Convert the **frequency reading 2425 MHz** to **Gigahertz.**
Move the decimal left three positions: **2425 MHz = 2.425 GHz.**

We'll revisit this kind of math prefix conversion and decimal shifting in Section 8.3 with some electrical measurements, so keep that goofism handy!

Amplitude: Remember when you were out in the ocean at the start of this section, bobbing up and down as the waves and sharks rolled by? Your position at the high point of the wave or at the low trough, as measured from the middle height of the wave, is the *amplitude* of the wave. You can think of amplitude in two ways: 1) it is the height of the wave as measured from the middle, or the maximum "size" of the electric or magnetic field; and 2) it is the *power* of the radio signal. Hence, a low amplitude represented by a short waveform means low signal power. A high amplitude, or tall waveform, represents high signal power. Radio wave power, or amplitude, can be varied to encode a signal, and that is *amplitude modulation*, or AM radio as we saw way back in Section 1.1. (Refer to AM or SSB modulation, Figure 1.3 on page 13.)

Polarization: Also as noted before, a radio wave's electric field component and magnetic field component oscillate with the wave in a specific orientation, or direction. Radio wave polarization refers to the direction of oscillation, and the electric field direction is the reference used. Remember, identical polarization is important for strong signal reception, as a pair of "cross polarized" antennas are not very efficient. Vertical, horizontal, circular, and random polarizations are used in amateur radio. (Refer to polarization, Figure 1.9.)

Phase Relationships: In the course of one wavelength an exact position within the up-down or side-to-side cycle is called the phase of the wave. In mathematics the phase is described as an angle between 0 and 360 degrees, just like a circle. Beginning at the axis of propagation with 0 degrees, the wave increases to maximum amplitude at 90 degrees, returns back to the axis half way through the cycle at 180 degrees, continues to the most negative value (below the axis) at 270 degrees, and finally completes the cycle back up to the axis at 360 degrees – where it starts all over again with the next wave cycle.

Two waveforms of equal wavelength have a *phase relationship* with one another that is described in terms of the difference in degrees between the two waves. For instance, one wave may be considered "behind" another wave by 180 degrees if the two waves are oscillating exactly opposite directions of one another. If this occurs, the electric field of the first wave will be positive when the second wave's field is a negative (opposite direction) value of the same magnitude. If the waves' electric fields are added together, such as when an antenna detects both waveforms simultaneously, the net signal strength at the antenna will be zero! The perfectly out-of-phase waves cancel out one another. Other phase relationships result in different field strength sums. Phase relationships are important to understanding many concepts in radio wave propagation.

Figure 4.4 on the next page illustrates the 180 degree "out of phase" relationship and a 90 degree phase relationship.

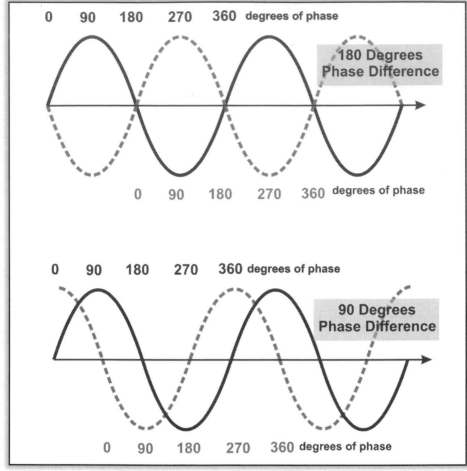

Figure 4.4: Waveform Phase Relationships

Shazaam! That's pretty cosmic stuff, huh? Don't hesitate to reread this section a few times if the concepts of electromagnetic waves and frequencies are foreign to you. When you're at least semi-comfortable with it, get online and try the question pool's **Section 4.1** exam questions. They're not as scary as sharks and they're less sneaky than crabs! Good luck, and get going!

www.HamRadioSchool.com/tech_media

\

4.2 Bands, Band Plans, & License Privileges

Wavelength, Frequency, & Bands

" *Have you considered that if you don't make waves, nobody including yourself will know that you are alive? – Theodore Isaac Rubin*

One reason all that wavelength and frequency stuff is important is because that is how the FCC defines the various segments of the radio spectrum on which hams are allowed to transmit, and because hams use those designations in every-day discussion. And even within an FCC designated frequency band there are *sub-bands*, again defined by the frequency range, on which only certain modes of transmission are allowed or on which some license classes are prohibited. Commonly, detailed band plans are locally coordinated to define frequency ranges for specific operations, such as simplex voice, repeater frequency pairs, digital modes, and even for experimental purposes.

So, in order to understand such *band plans*, the limitations of your license privileges, and to avoid accidentally interfering with other stations, you should understand the FCC amateur radio band plan and your local frequency co-ordination band plans. **Beyond the privileges established by the FCC, a band plan is a voluntary guideline for using different modes or activities within an amateur band.** That is, the FCC band plan is regulation, while locally coordinated plans are voluntary recommendations.

T2A10

I know, it sounds complicated, but you'll warm up to band plans quickly once you begin using your radio. Study the Amateur Band Plan extracts presented in this section and the full FCC amateur plan on our web site, and it'll begin to make more sense to you. Then you can *make waves* properly, *feeling alive* and letting it be known to everyone else on the air!

HF, VHF, UHF: The broadest categories of the most common amateur RF transmissions are *High Frequency* (HF), *Very High Frequency* (VHF), and *Ultra High Frequency* (UHF). Each is a specific range of frequencies.

HF: 3 to 30 MHz
VHF: 30 to 300 MHz
UHF: 300 to 3000 MHz

T3B10 T3B09 T3B08

Notice how these are each bounded by a '3' number, only with different quantities of zeros following. It is easy to remember that way; just adding zeros behind the 3's to get the boundary of each range of frequencies. And all are in units of megahertz (MHz).

You should be aware that there are several additional categories, from extremely low frequency (ELF) to *extremely high frequency* (EHF). Amateurs do have privileges from medium frequency (MF) to EFH, but HF, VHF, and UHF are, by far, the most commonly used ranges.

Amateur Frequency Bands: Within each of the broad categories of HF, VHF, and UHF are narrower ranges of frequencies that have been allocated for amateur use. These are the bands that amateurs tend to identify by the approximate wavelength associated with the band frequencies. Remember, you can calculate a frequency from a wavelength, and vice versa, as we did in the last section. Using the calculation you can usually figure out what band a frequency belongs to.

Examples: **If you are transmitting on 223.50 MHz...**

T1B07

300 ÷ 223.50 MHz = 1.34 meters wavelength

The closest amateur band to 1.34 meters is the **1.25 meter band**, and that's the band where 223.50 MHz resides.

But sometimes you need to have a little more knowledge of the band plans. Take a look at this exam pool question:

Q. Which frequency is within the 6 meter band?

T1B03

| A. 49.00 MHz | **B. 52.525 MHz** |
| C. 28.50 MHz | D. 222.15 MHz |

Performing the calculation 300 ÷ 6 = 50.0 MHz. But the closest answer, 49.00 MHz, is incorrect! The 6 meter band ranges 50.0 to 54.0 MHz. So, it pays to be familiar with the boundaries of the bands for this reason. In the other exam question cases the closest numerical answer to the calculation is always the correct response. Remember, these are *approximate* wavelength names in *meters*! In these last example questions, the band is expressed in *centimeters*.

Q. Which 70 cm frequency is authorized to a Technician Class license holder operating in ITU Region 2? (300 ÷ 0.70 m = 428.57 MHz).

T1B05

| A. 53.350 MHz | B. 146.52 MHz |
| **C. 443.350 MHz** | D. 222.520 MHz |

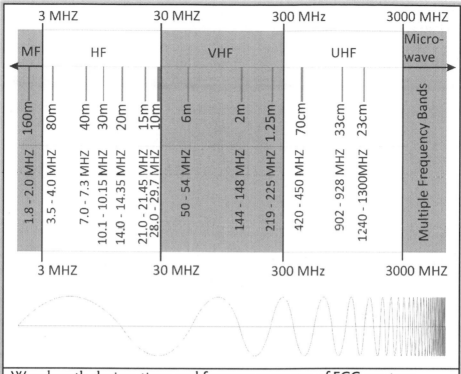

Wavelength designations and frequency ranges of FCC amateur bands. Not depicted: 12m, 17m, & 60m bands, higher UHF bands, and detailed microwave bands. Note upper/lower frequency scale is logarithmic (10x).

Figure 4.5: Amateur Bands within HF, VHF, & UHF Regions

Q. Which 23 cm frequency is authorized to a Technician Class licensee? (300 ÷ 0.23 m = 1304 MHz)

A. 2315 MHz   **B. 1296 MHz**
C. 3390 MHz   D. 146.52 MHz

T1B06

Sub-Bands: There are several questions in the pool about sub-bands, and while you can always look them up on a chart you have to know them for the exam. In particular you should familiarize yourself with which Technician license bands have *mode restricted sub-bands*. Mode restricted means that you may use only certain transmission modes in those sub-bands, such as CW-only or digital-only modes. Be sure you know where the CW-only and data-only (digital mode-only) sub-bands are located within the Technician

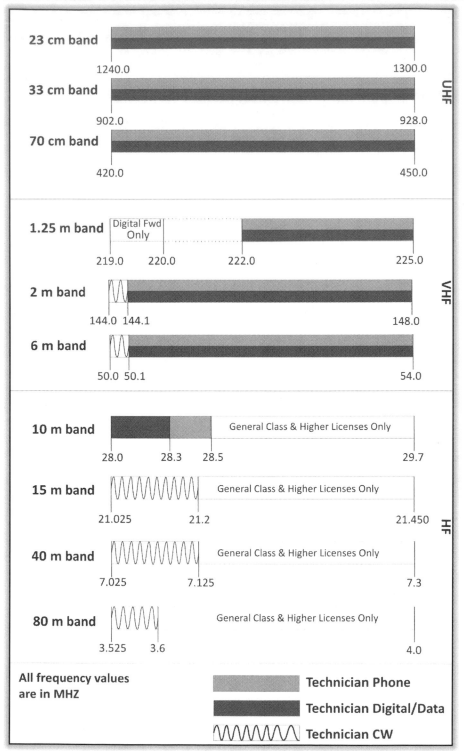

Figure 4.6: Technician Band Privileges

bands. At frequencies **above 30 MHz, Technician class operators have mode-restricted sub-bands in the 6 meter, 2 meter, and 1.25 meter bands,** as well as in the 10 meter HF band.

Technician License Privileges: In accordance with the FCC amateur band plan, each license class has specific frequency privileges. License privileges expand with the higher license classes, General and Amateur Extra. However, your Technician license privileges provide a tremendous breadth of opportunities to experience the variety of activities available in amateur radio. Reference Figure 4.6 page as you read about the Technician license phone, CW, and digital/data privileges.

Technician Phone (voice) Privileges: As a Technician licensee you have phone mode privileges In VHF and UHF equivalent to those of General and Amateur Extra licensees! There are no Technician restrictions beyond the FCC plan except for your locally coordinated band plans that you should follow. So, you have full phone access to: 6m band, 2m band, 1.25m band, 70 cm band, and higher frequency bands, as shown in Figure 4.6. (Note: Technicians also have privileges in higher UHF bands and microwave bands that are less commonly used and are not depicted in Figure 4.6.)

While most phone privileges in the VHF and UHF bands implies FM voice mode, you should be aware that **single sideband (SSB) phone mode is permitted in at least some portion of all the amateur bands above 50 MHz** (6 meter band and higher frequency bands). Locally coordinated band plans will usually designate sub-bands for SSB operations separate from FM operations. Because of its efficient use of power, SSB is a popular mode for contesting in VHF and UHF bands. (More on SSB coming in Chapter 6.)

In the HF range the Technician phone privileges are restricted to the 10m band only, and specifically a 200 kHz sub-band between 28.300 – 28.500 MHz. On the lower HF frequency bands, 12m to 160m, Technicians have no phone privileges. Upgrade to General license to use those bands!

Technician CW Privileges: Technician licensees have CW privileges in the VHF 6m and 2m bands, and in the low frequency portions of 10m, 15m, 40m, and 80m bands. **On 6m band emissions are restricted to CW-only in the mode-restricted sub-band 50.0 – 50.1 MHz. Similarly on 2m band emissions are restricted to CW-only in the sub-band 144.0 – 144.1 MHz.** Notice that CW sub-bands are all in the lowest frequency part of each band. Additionally, CW is considered a digital/data mode, so Technicians may also transmit CW in digital/data bands depicted in Figure 4.6.

T1B10

T2B13

T1B11

Technician Digital / Data Privileges: Technicians may use digital transmission modes all across the VHF and UHF bands, such as 6m, 2m, 1.25m, 70cm, and higher bands, except where CW-only restricted. (Check your locally coordinated band plan for additional restrictions on digital / data transmissions.) Additionally, Technicians may use digital or data modes in the lowest frequencies of the HF 10m band, 28.000 – 28.300 MHz. **Note that a unique data-only emission mode sub-band exists between 219 and 220 MHz** in the 1.25m band for fixed digital message forwarding systems (email, APRS, etc. – See Chapter 10).

Secondary Privileges: Some bands or sub-bands may be available for amateur use only on a *secondary basis*. As noted in Section 2.4, **amateur service is secondary in some portions of the 70 cm band. This means that amateurs may find non-amateur stations in the bands and must avoid interfering with them.** Avoid transmitting near frequencies in use by primary users and leave the frequency or cease your operations if requested by a primary user. (Also, see the FCC Amateur Radio Band Plan notes regarding the 160m, 60m, 40m, and 30m bands.)

Study the ARRL FCC band plan chart on the web site and focus on the Technician privileges that are designated by the 'T' in the letters to the right of each band. And pay attention to the color or pattern codes, noting phone, data, and CW privileges. It won't take long to see the pattern of mode use and license privileges, even if the frequency values are not second nature yet. Give it time and that will come. You'll be spouting off bands and frequencies like an old elmer in no time!

And remember: When you are just getting started with FM operations and you are using 2m, 1.25m, or 70cm repeaters or simplex channels, you are safely within your license privileges and coordinated band plan usage. Have no fear! Make lots of waves!

Time for questions! Log on, check out the FCC band plan chart, and tackle the questions for **Section 4.2**. Good luck!

www.HamRadioSchool.com/tech_media

5.0 Signal Propagation

> **❝ The electromagnetic waves are literally sky-scrapers in as much as they touch the ionosphere and are reflected from it. — Peter Redgrove**

[handwritten annotations: Thermosphere; 50-250mi Ionosphere; Mesosphere; — Stratosphere; 0-6mi — Troposphere]

Up to now we've focused quite a lot on VHF and UHF communications with simplex or repeater operations via strong signals. Now we're going to jump into a topic that still applies to the VHF frequencies, but is absolutely the heart and soul of HF communications around the world where we are transmitting and receiving weak signals. So, we're going to climb upon those *electromagnetic skyscrapers* now and stretch your radio horizons!

Propagation refers to the spreading or traveling of radio waves through the atmosphere or free space. Different RF frequencies have different propagation characteristics, being affected by the atmosphere and environment in different ways. The various characteristics of propagation may be typed roughly along the HF, VHF, and UHF frequency categories, so we will consider each frequency range in turn and examine the factors impacting propagation.

HF Propagation

Ionosphere: The high frequency bands (160m – 10m) are readily bent or refracted by layers of electrically charged particles called ions high in the atmosphere. Collectively these layers are known as the ionosphere. The strength of this bending effect varies with frequency and with the densities of the ionosphere's different layers.

Sky Wave or Skip: Signals that are bent back to earth by the ionosphere are sometimes called "sky wave" propagation or "skip." **The ionosphere enables the propagation of radio signals around the world** with multiple reflections between the ionosphere and earth. Generally, longer wavelengths (lower frequencies) are refracted more readily than shorter wavelengths (higher frequencies). The ionosphere bends lower frequency signals more than it bends higher frequency signals.

T3A11

Skip Signal Polarization: As a radio signal moves into the ionosphere the electromagnetic field of the waveform is affected by the ionosphere's charged particles and by the earth's magnetic field. Imagine the nicely oscillating waveform, as depicted in Figures 1.9 and 4.3, beginning to rotate around as it propagates forward. The polarization of the wave, normally defined by the direction of the electric field oscillation, is now changing from moment to moment as the waveform twists along like a corkscrew! This spinning polarization resulting from propagation through the ionosphere is called *elliptical polarization*. **The result is that either vertically or horizontally polarized antennas may be used for transmission or reception of these elliptically polarized signals refracted from the ionosphere.** The polarization of skip signals becomes randomized and essentially irrelevant, and they will be weaker than signals well-matched to antenna polarization.

T3A09

Signal Fade: Also common with skip propagation is **irregular fading of signals received by ionospheric reflection.** This fluctuation in signal strength is **caused by random combining of signals arriving via different paths,** thereby causing them to interfere in constructive or destructive ways, as the phase relationships shift among the multiple paths.

T3A08

Ionosphere Diurnal Cycle: The ionosphere's charged particles are created by the sun's radiation when high energy light rays strip electrons from atoms high in the atmosphere. More sunlight and more sunspot activity results in more ions, or a denser and more effective ionosphere. The density and arrangement of layers of the ionosphere change with the day-night cycle of the earth (diurnal cycle), with a general reduction in density and effectiveness for bending radio signals at night.

Layers of Ionosphere: The ionosphere exhibits four distinct layers designated from low to high altitude as: D Layer, E Layer, F1 Layer, and F2 Layer. On the night side of the earth, while in darkness, the high F1 and F2 layers merge into a single F Layer. The E Layer weakens significantly at night, and the low altitude D Layer typically disappears entirely at night. These daily cyclical changes cause variations in the skip propagation behavior of different HF frequencies.

Upper HF Bands: The higher HF frequency bands such as 10m, 12m, 15m, 17m, 20m, will be bent most significantly by the dense F1 and F2 Layers, which are the highest altitude layers. Thus, these shorter wavelength bands tend to propagate long distances due to the high altitude of the layers from which they are typically reflected, particularly in daylight hours when the F layers are dense and highly activated. However,

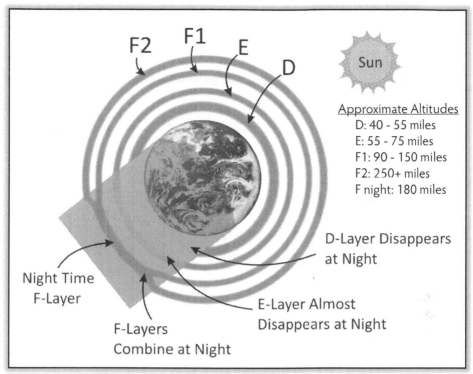

Figure 5.1: Diurnal Cycle of the Ionosphere

the E layer will sometimes also bend the higher frequencies when it is activated, particularly the 10m band.

Lower HF Bands: The lower frequency HF bands such as 40m, 60m, 80m, 160m, tend to be absorbed by the ion charges of the D layer. As a result, these bands do not achieve good skip propagation during the day. When the D Layers dissipate at night these low frequency HF bands may then be bent very effectively by the high altitude combined F-layer that endures through the night. So, at night the low frequency bands reach higher ionospheric layers where the skip distances are greater and their long distance propagation is enhanced.

Solar Cycles and Effects: The ionosphere is ionized to various degrees by the variable output of the sun and by the day-night cycle. Sunspots are regions on the face of the sun that produce a lot of ultraviolet radiation (UV), and UV radiation produces ions in the earth's ionosphere. Thus, the ionosphere is most densely charged with ions during periods of high sunspot activity and especially on the daylight side of the earth. Sunspots vary in number and intensity over an 11-year cycle of the sun. This has big effects on radio skip propagation!

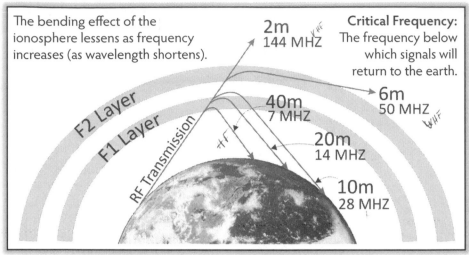

The bending effect of the ionosphere lessens as frequency increases (as wavelength shortens).

2m
144 MHZ

Critical Frequency: The frequency below which signals will return to the earth.

F2 Layer

F1 Layer

RF Transmission

40m
7 MHZ

6m
50 MHZ

20m
14 MHZ

10m
28 MHZ

Figure 5.2: Ionosphere Effects by Frequency

For instance, because the 10m band is the highest frequency HF amateur band, the ionosphere's bending effect on its frequencies is weaker than for the lower bands. The ionosphere density is not always sufficient to bend 10m signals back to earth. **Generally, the best time for long-distance 10 meter band propagation via the F layer is from dawn to shortly after sunset during periods of high sunspot activity. During the peak of the sunspot cycle, 6m band and 10m band may provide long distance communications** by skip propagation.

Of course, 10m is of great interest to all Technicians since this is where the license provides HF phone privileges! In the mornings during high sunspot activity you will be able to skip to the east better, so European stations will be within reach from the US. In the afternoon the west opens up and the Pacific nations are popular. The longer skip distances tend to be up to 2,500 miles per bounce, and closer stations *inside the bounce* may not be heard.

VHF Propagation

The VHF bands (6m, 2m, 1.25m) are less susceptible to the ionosphere's bending effects because signal frequencies are higher than HF. Usually, VHF signals are *above the critical frequency*, meaning that they are not bent sufficiently to return them to the earth's surface. But occasionally VHF signals are bent back to earth when the E-Layer is very active with charged particles. VHF frequencies may also be affected by other atmospheric phenomena besides the ionosphere, carrying your signals long distances!

Multi-mode Radio: Signals propagating over long distances become weak, and some operating modes work better than others for weak signal communications. Single sideband mode is one popular weak signal mode, and CW's narrow bandwidth works particularly well. **A multi-mode VHF transceiver is a device that is most useful for VHF weak signal communication!** Multi-mode transceivers will typically provide FM, SSB, AM, and many have accommodations for CW and digital modes.

Sporadic E: The ionosphere E-Layer effect is very dynamic or sporadic, often changing significantly in strength or effect in a matter of seconds to minutes. Patches of the E-Layer can become quite dense with ions and be very effective with even relatively short VHF wavelengths. Thus, when the E-Layer is very active **strong over-the-horizon signals on 10m, 6m, and 2m are most commonly associated with E-Layer signal refraction called "Sporadic E." When VHF signals are being received from long distances, they might be refracted from a sporadic E layer.**

Tropospheric Ducting: When warm air masses move above cool air masses in the lowest layer of the atmosphere to create **a temperature inversion,** an effective pipe or "duct" is formed in the troposphere that may propagate VHF frequencies hundreds of miles over the horizon.

Tropospheric Scatter: Some VHF (and UHF) frequencies may be randomly scattered near the top of the troposphere. **This allows over-the-horizon VHF and UHF communications to ranges up to 300 miles on a regular basis.** This weak signal scatter is cause by small particles high in the troposphere such as water, volcanic ash, or dust.

Auroral Reflection: The Northern Lights or aurora, are also charged particles in the atmosphere that can bend VHF signals back to the earth. Aurora are very dynamic, and **the characteristic of VHF signals received via auroral reflection is rapid fluctuations of strength and often sound distorted.** The 6m band tends to be most effective for aurora reflection.

Meteor Scatter: The 6m band is best suited to communicating via meteor scatter, in which signals are reflected off of the atmospheric ionization that trails behind meteors as they enter the atmosphere. These communications are usually a very brief exchange of call signs that last for only a few seconds until the meteor's ionized trail dissipates.

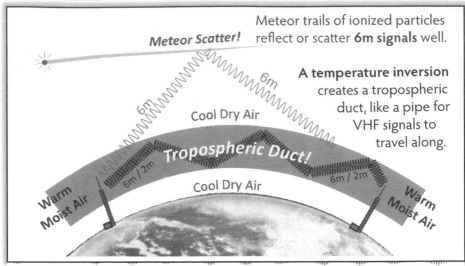

Figure 5.3: Tropospheric Ducting & Meteor Scatter

UHF Propagation

T3C01 **The ultra high frequency bands (70 cm – 23 cm and higher) are usually not reflected by the ionosphere. UHF signals are rarely heard from stations outside your local coverage area.** UHF frequencies may be affected by tropospheric scatter, as noted under VHF Propagation.

T3C05 **Knife Edge Diffraction: Can cause radio signals to be heard despite obstructions between the transmitting and receiving stations.** Signals are partially bent around solid objects exhibiting sharp edges. Knife edge effects around buildings or over mountain peaks can help direct radio signals over the horizon or around obstacles.

Like I said, *stretching your radio horizons.* Get it? Once you have your Technician license you can get on 10m band and try your hand at ionospheric skip. You can make contacts around the globe, sometimes with just a few watts of power. It's a great HF band, and with the sun very active and firing up the F layers, it is a load of fun!

Sporadic E can be very exciting as well, if less reliable. Sporadic E tends to become more common about twice during the year, in June and in January. Listen for those sporadic E opportunities and capitalize on some long distance contacts. VHF contesting gets really fun with sporadic E!

But for now, go snag those exam pool questions for **Section 5.0.**
www.HamRadioSchool.com/tech_media

| 6.0 | How Radio Works |

> **" Knowing how things work is the basis for appreciation, and is thus a source of civilized delight. — William Safire**

I know you have a burning question within you, begging for a sane and sensible response in common language we can all understand: *How does radio really work?*

This chapter will temporarily sate your thirst for knowledge of radio's inner workings. *Temporarily*, because once you have digested this introduction to radio's secrets it will likely make you crave even more detailed understanding of RF magic. Ready yourself for major infusion of civilized radio delight!

This chapter contains some challenging technical concepts, but we will tackle them with simplified explanations and build one thing upon another. A greater amount of background explanation is provided here than in other chapters, but this extra background will provide a solid foundation for comprehending the innards and functions of your radio. It will also help make the exam questions about these topics seem delightfully easy!

The Big Picture: Here is an overview of the big picture we will paint in the three sections of this chapter:

1. Your voice is made of many different sound tones that form a band of sonic frequencies. (A continuous range of frequencies.)
2. The radio microphone converts the band of sound frequencies into an equivalent band of audio electrical signals that contain the sound wave information of your voice.
3. The audio electrical signals are used to shape, or modulate, an equivalent band of radio frequency (RF) signals so that they contain the audio signal information within them.
4. The band of RF signals is sent from the transmitter to be radiated into space by the antenna.
5. A receiving antenna captures the RF band signals and sends them to the receiver electronic circuits.

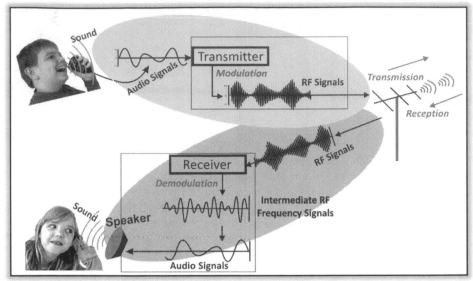

Figure 6.1: Transceiver Big Picture

6. The receiver circuits recreate the audio band signals from the modulated RF band signals in a series of steps that convert the higher radio frequencies into lower radio frequencies and finally into even lower frequency audio electrical signals. (Demodulation process.)

7. The extracted (demodulated) audio signals are fed to a speaker to recreate the original voice sounds.

Quite a lot of detail can be unfolded from that series of events that describes exactly how your radio works. Let the unfolding begin!

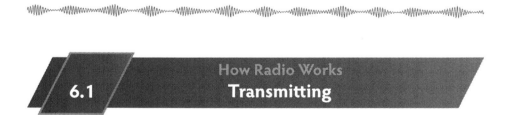

How Radio Works
6.1   Transmitting

CW **Transmission:** The simplest transmission mode is CW, or continuous wave transmissions. Recall that CW uses only an unmodulated steady signal that is interrupted in patterns to convey a message, and Morse Code is the most common 'pattern' used in amateur radio with CW mode.

A simple CW transmitter has these components as shown in Figure 6.2:

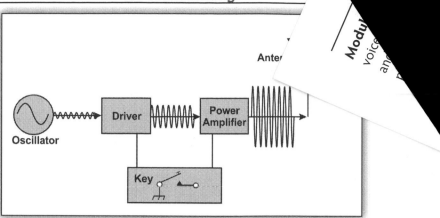

Figure 6.2: CW Transmitter Block Diagram

- **Oscillator: The oscillator is a circuit that generates a signal of a desired frequency,** perhaps many megahertz. Remember, this signal is an electrical alternating current surging back and forth, and it is routed to the driver component of the CW transmitter.

- **Driver:** The driver is a type of amplifier that boosts the amplitude (power) of the relatively weak RF signal generated by the oscillator.

- **Power Amplifier:** The power amplifier receives the oscillating signal from the driver, boosts its power further, and outputs the signal to the antenna.

- **Key:** The key, or telegraph key, is a switch that controls whether the continuous wave signal is passed or interrupted between the driver and power amplifier. The key is the control an operator uses to send the patterns of Morse Code.

- **Antenna:** As the strongly amplified alternating current (AC) surges back and forth in the antenna much of its power is converted into electromagnetic radiation of a frequency equal to the AC frequency.

Thus, an RF signal is transmitted from the antenna when the key is closed, completing the circuit and allowing the alternating electrical current to energize the antenna. On the other end of the communication another antenna will be energized by the radio waves impinging on its elements, converting them back into alternating electrical currents that are conducted down the antenna feedline (cable). A radio receiver will convert these recreated AC signals into an audio frequency signal that is emitted by a speaker as a consistent tone. This way, the Morse Code signal can be heard by the receiving radio operator as a pattern of tones. That is basic transmission, but there's a lot more! Now let's see how your voice is included in a transmission.

ated Phone Transmission: Phone modes transmit the sound of your
by radio waves. When you push-to-talk you power up the microphone
you activate the transmitter. The sound waves detected by the micro-
hone are encoded into radio frequency transmissions. This encoding process
is called *modulation*. Let's start our modulation journey with some important
background about sound and microphones.

Sound: Sound is our perception of mechanical waves in the air. Just as ocean
waves need the medium of water to travel, sound needs the medium of air.

Sound waves are the *compression* and *rarefaction* of air molecules moving
across a distance. The molecules get squeezed tightly together in the compressions and they get spread far apart in the rarefactions. A loud sound will have
densely compacted air compression areas and thinly populated air rarefaction
areas. A soft sound will have only mild differences in the density of molecules
across the wave. We say these variations in molecule densities are variations in
air pressure, or *sound pressure*. The magnitude of the difference in a wave's
sound pressure is its amplitude.

Voice: Your voice is a blend of many different sound frequencies. Depending
on your individual vocal chords the low vowel sounds, such as the 'o' sound at
the end of the word 'radio,' may contain frequencies around 200 Hz.

The hard consonant sounds such as those of D, T, P, or Ch, contain much higher
frequencies, perhaps near 2,500 Hz or higher. And there are many more in
between. Most voices can be clearly produced with a continuous range of
about 3,000 different sound frequencies, or 3,000 Hz.

Microphone: Your radio microphone detects a range of sound frequencies made by your voice and converts those into AC electrical signals, usually called *audio* signals. These audio frequency signals will vary in voltage
the same way the sound waves vary with your voice: Make a loud sound and
the amplitude of the voltage signals becomes greater; make the pitch of
your voice go high and the frequencies of the voltage signals get higher too
(shorter wavelengths). Figure 6.3 illustrates sound waves converted into audio
electrical signals by a microphone. The microphone performs this conversion
for the many different frequencies of your voice all at once, creating many different audio electrical frequency signals simultaneously.

Notice in the figure that the electrical audio signals produced by the microphone are depicted as squiggly waveforms in which the voltage oscillates from
+v to –v. The pointing arrow of the horizontal axis represents the passage of
time; as you move along the axis you are seeing different points in time. Every
point on the squiggly waveform represents the direction and magnitude

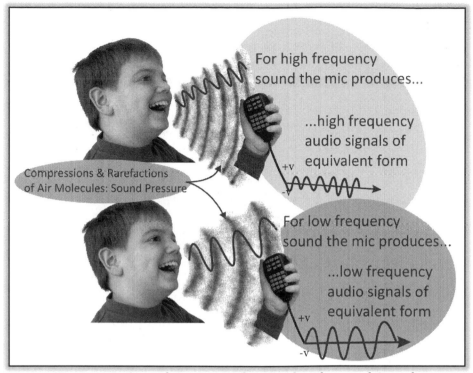

Figure 6.3: Sound Converted to Audio Electrical Signals

(strength) of the signal voltage at the given point in time on the axis. The +v and −v voltages simply indicate opposite directions of the voltage force in the microphone's AC signal.

The voltage force pushes electrons in the '+' direction up to some +v maximum force, then it reduces in strength back to zero at the axis. The voltage continues by reversing its force to the '−' direction, again reaching a maximum force of −v, then subsiding back to zero again at the axis. Repeat. Repeat. Repeat. This back-and-forth voltage occurs with the same regularity as the sound frequency of your voice that it is representing – the same as the air wave compressions and rarefactions produced by the sound of your voice. Note, these AC signals are of much lower frequency than RF, hundreds or thousands of hertz rather than the millions or hundreds of millions of hertz we have considered in the amateur radio frequency bands.

A depiction like the squiggly line electrical signals of Figure 6.3, in which time runs along the horizontal axis and the signal strength is depicted as up-and-down squiggly lines, is a "time domain" view of a signal. (Keep that in mind, and we will examine a different but related view in a moment!)

Audio Band: Remember, the microphone is creating a varying voltage signal like the time domain depiction for each of the many different frequencies of your voice. As depicted in Figure 6.4, you may imagine the microphone's audio signals as a set of about 3,000 waveforms, low to high frequency, each with a rapidly alternating voltage level over time, and the set of them accurately copying the variations among the 3,000 sound waveforms of your voice.

We call this set of electrical signals representing your voice the *audio band*. Because it is comprised of a band of about 3,000 frequencies we say it has a bandwidth of 3,000 Hz (or 3.0 kHz). In the 3D view of Figure 6.4 you can imagine viewing straight down the frequency axis and getting a time domain view, like the squiggly microphone waveform depiction of Figure 6.3.

Alternatively, if you view down the time axis straight onto the band of frequencies, you will get a "frequency domain" view. The frequency domain view depicts the amplitude (height) of each waveform in the band from low to high frequency values. The amplitude represents the power (or sound loudness) for each frequency in the band. You may have seen an audio stereo equalizer display like this in which the display indicators jump up and down across the band of frequencies as music is played. That equalizer display is a frequency domain view. (Note: Since it would get a little crowded trying to depict almost

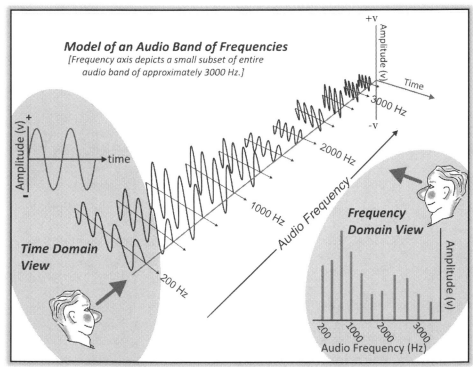

Figure 6.4: Envisioning the Audio Band

3,000 frequencies of the audio band, an interval subset of audio frequencies is depicted in our frequency domain view of Figure 6.4.)

We will use both time domain and frequency domain views throughout this chapter and on the *HamRadioSchool.com* web site to describe how radio works, so study these graphs closely!

Microphone Gain: For each of the frequencies in the audio band the microphone produces a small squiggly voltage signal that is proportional to the sound pressure levels. These low power signals are delivered to a signal amplifier that boosts them to greater voltage levels that can be used by the radio transmitter. The ratio of increase in the signal levels produced by the microphone amplifier is the microphone's *gain*. You can imagine that the amplifier could really boost the signals a lot and produce very large changes in the oscillating voltages of the signals (high gain), or it could increase them only slightly to produce mild proportional increases in the signal amplitude (low gain).

If a transmitter is operated with the microphone gain set too high, the output signal might become distorted. *Clipping* of the audio signal is one type of distortion possible from too high gain, as depicted in Figure 6.5. A signal is clipped when the maximum output voltage level of the microphone amplifier is reached before the microphone's input signal has achieved its maximum amplitude. Shouting loudly or speaking too close to a microphone can cause clipping distortion.

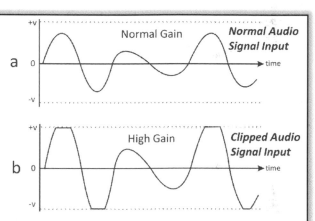

Audio signals 'a' and 'b' are identical except that 'b' is of greater amplitude due to high microphone amplifier gain. In 'b' the maximum output signal limit is reached, "clipping" the signal peaks and distorting the audio.

Figure 6.5: Excessive Microphone Gain

Amplitude Modulation (AM): The encoding of information into radio frequency signals is *modulation*. In a phone mode the information to be encoded is the sound of your voice, now represented by the audio band electrical signals, boosted by the microphone amplifier. The radio transmitter must now create radio signals that represent these audio band signals.

Remember, the radio frequency signals are typically many millions of hertz (MHz), while the audio signals are typically only a few hundred to a few thousand hertz. The much higher frequency (shorter wavelength) RF signals can be "shaped" to mimic the much lower frequency (longer wavelength) audio signals. In AM, the amplitude of an RF signal is shaped to mimic the amplitude of an audio signal. The following is a somewhat simplified version of how this is done by the transmitter so that the many various frequencies of your voice are carried by the radio waves.

Audio Band to RF Band: Each of the approximately 3,000 audio band frequencies is assigned a unique radio frequency counterpart to represent it. There is a one-to-one matching of audio-to-RF frequencies. So, when you PTT you are transmitting a band of a few thousand different radio frequencies that are near the frequency to which you have tuned the radio. You are not transmitting just that single tuned frequency!

The tuned frequency value on the radio display is called the *carrier frequency*. The carrier is a reference frequency value that is used to calculate a unique RF band counterpart frequency for each of the audio band frequencies delivered from the microphone. Figure 6.6a depicts a frequency domain view of the one-to-one matching of the audio band frequencies to an RF band's frequencies within the 10m amateur band (28 MHz range). This RF domain depicts one AM *sideband,* meaning that this RF band of counterpart frequencies is all on one side of the carrier frequency – in this example, the sideband frequencies are all higher than (above) the carrier frequency of 28.4 MHz.

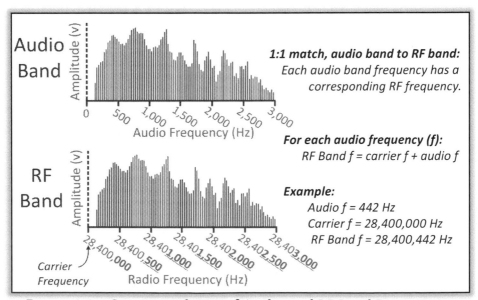

Figure 6.6a: Correspondence of Audio and RF Band Frequencies

Notice that in the RF sideband of Figure 6.6a each RF frequency is calculated by adding the counterpart audio frequency to the carrier frequency value. Performing this simple addition for each of the approximately 3,000 audio frequencies determines the band of RF frequencies that will be transmitted in this sideband. Notice also that the amplitude of each RF sideband frequency mimics the amplitude of its counterpart audio frequency. So, the shape of the frequency bands is identical, with the RF band copying the audio band over the time of transmission. If these were two stereo equalizer displays they would be dancing in synchrony, only different in frequency values by a few million hertz! Now let's see how that dancing act is accomplished for each one of the nearly 3,000 frequencies in the bands.

Envelopes: Now reference the Figure 6.6b time domain depiction of a single frequency out of the 3,000 Hz band. The audio signal shape and its amplitude mirror image are used to control the '+v' and the '−v' values of its much higher radio frequency counterpart. The enclosing "shape" of the audio signal amplitude, called the *envelope,* is imposed on the radio frequency amplitude over time. The amplitude of the RF signal increases and decreases over the transmission time exactly as dictated by its audio signal counterpart, even though the RF oscillates at a much higher frequency "inside the envelope." But unlike the low audio frequency, the higher RF may be radiated and effectively

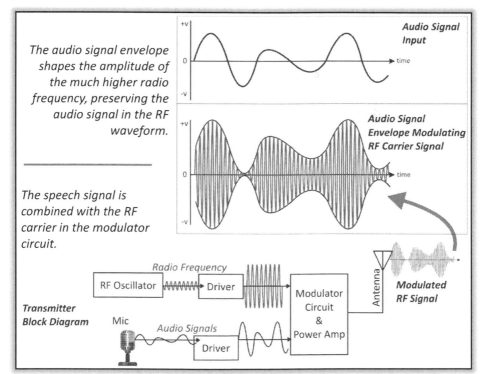

Figure 6.6b: Modulating RF Signals with an Audio Envelope

transmitted through space, carrying the audio waveform information along. An identical process occurs for each of the nearly 3,000 Hz of audio frequencies and each uniquely calculated counterpart RF band frequency. Thus proceeds the amplitude modulation dance!

Modulator Circuit: The lower portion of Figure 6.6b depicts an amplitude modulation transmitter block diagram. Notice that the upper path of the transmitter sequence is almost identical to the CW transmitter of Figure 6.2. The oscillator circuit produces the RF carrier signal that is combined with your audio signals in the amplitude modulation process. The lower path in the block diagram represents the audio signal creation, amplification, and combining with the RF carrier signal. **Modulation, described by the combining of your speech with an RF carrier signal,** is accomplished in the modulator circuit part of the transmitter as shown in the block diagram.

T7A08

AM Transmission: Finally, the entire band of amplitude modulated RF signals is radiated from the antenna as in Figure 6.6c, but this band is not alone! With true AM, a sideband above the carrier is transmitted just as in our example, but another entire sideband of frequencies *below* the carrier is also transmitted, and the carrier frequency itself is transmitted. The sideband frequencies below the carrier are calculated by subtracting each audio frequency from the carrier value rather than adding to it, as in our previous 10m band example of Figure 6.6a. This results in a mirror image sideband on

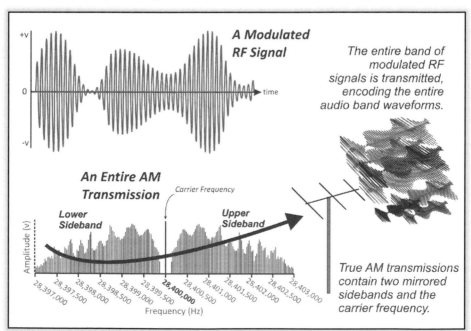

Figure 6.6c: Transmitting the AM Band of Modulated RF Frequencies

the lower side of the carrier doing the modulation dance too! True AM is a robust, if dual-redundant and somewhat power-inefficient, phone mode.

We will examine AM transmission and its skinny dancing cousin, *single side-band transmission*, a bit more closely in Section 6.3. For now let's venture briefly into the world of frequency modulation (FM) transmission.

FM Phone Modulation: Frequency modulation works differently than AM. Rather than making changes to the amplitude of RF signals to encode the audio signals, the frequency of an RF signal is changed as dictated by the audio band signal amplitude. You were introduced to the FM mode basic concept back in Section 1.3.

Deviation: Notice in the FM time domain depiction of Figure 6.7 the RF carrier frequency increases (shorter wavelengths) as the audio signal amplitude increases, and the RF carrier frequency decreases (longer wavelengths) as the audio amplitude decreases. When the audio signal amplitude is at zero, the associated RF carrier frequency value is known as the *resting frequency.* The change in the RF carrier frequency from its resting frequency is called the frequency *deviation.* Using this terminology we may state the fact that **the amount of deviation of an FM signal is determined by the amplitude of the modulating signal.** (The audio signal is the modulating signal.)

T2B05

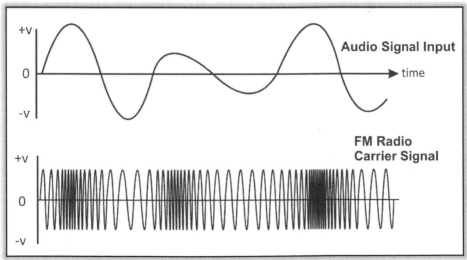

Figure 6.7: Revisiting Frequency Modulation

FM Spring Model: I like to think of the FM carrier waveform as a spring that has a preferred state of intermediate stretch (resting frequency). The carrier spring may be stretched further out than its preferred state, extending the distance between coils (deviated to a lower frequency, longer wavelength form). The spring may also be compressed tighter than its preferred state, squeezing the coils closer together (deviated to a higher frequency, shorter wavelength form).

During FM transmission the carrier spring is constantly jittering back and forth between different amounts of extension or compression – variable magnitudes of frequency deviation from the resting frequency. As noted before, the amount of the extension and compression of the spring deviation is determined by the amplitude of the audio signal, as in Figure 6.8. So, speaking loudly into the microphone increases the audio signal amplitude and drives a large FM carrier deviation – big spring extensions and compressions. Remaining silent leaves the FM carrier at its resting frequency, with no deviation at all. Other sound levels in between these extremes produce intermediate levels of FM carrier deviation – intermediate magnitudes of extensions and compressions during the spring jittering.

FM Bandwidth: This leads to an interesting characteristic of FM transmission: **As the deviation of an FM transmitter is increased its signal occupies more bandwidth.** Remember, bandwidth is the range of the set of frequencies used in the transmission. As you speak louder the carrier frequency deviates across a wider range of frequencies, thereby using more bandwidth. FM uses variable amounts of bandwidth depending upon the loudness of your voice! (We will compare mode bandwidths in Section 6.3.)

T2B06

Over-Deviating: Similar to AM signal clipping, the carrier spring has limits to its stretching and compressing, or to its frequency deviation. When the modulating audio signal attempts to deviate the carrier beyond the normal limits of expansion or compression, the signal is said to be *over-deviating*. This causes distortion in the received audio, and it can be caused by speaking too closely or too loudly into the microphone. **Over-deviating is also caused by the microphone gain being too high, and it could cause your FM signal to interfere with stations on nearby frequencies** due to an extra-wide bandwidth signal being created by the excessive deviation. However, most modern FM transceivers include *limiters,* circuits that limit the transmitted band within a normal bandwidth range.

T2B07

FM Transmission: Now, let's take the spring model one step further. Each frequency in the audio band, from about 200 Hz to 3,000 Hz, is going to make the spring jitter at a rate equal to each of those different audio frequencies. For instance, the 200 Hz audio frequency is going to jitter the carrier spring

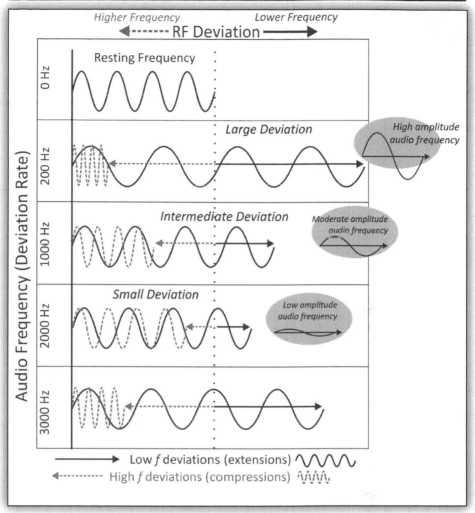

Figure 6.8: Spring Model of FM Carrier Deviation

at 200 times per second – the spring is extended and compressed 200 times each second. Similarly, the 2,500 Hz audio signal is going to extend and compress the spring 2,500 times each second. With FM, this is how the band of audio frequencies is represented, with a commensurate band of carrier spring jittering rates (a band of audio deviation frequencies).

Bringing it all together, each audio frequency is represented by the frequency of deviation of the RF carrier signal (the spring jitter rate), and an audio frequency's amplitude is represented by the magnitude of that deviation (the amount of extension and compression). So, you may think of the FM transmission as a set of carrier springs lined up in parallel as in Figure 6.8, each spring jittering at a different audio frequency, and each spring deviating by an amount proportional to the audio frequency amplitude, or loudness.

Keep in mind that like the previous AM description, the FM spring model is a simplification that omits some complex mathematics that more precisely describe the FM transmission signal. With FM the transmission signal gets very complicated, with all the various audio jittering frequencies piled upon one another in a wild and complex modulation dance. We have avoided both *Fourier Transforms* and *Bessel Functions* to gain a more intuitive way of thinking about AM and FM modulation. However, be aware in any more advanced learning about RF modulation you undertake that our intuitive models have limitations and do not precisely represent physical reality. They're a good start to really getting it, however!

For now, hit the question pool for **Section 6.1** and make sure you have the *transmitting* questions solidly understood. Then we will examine the other half of radio communications – receiving.

www.HamRadioSchool.com/tech_media

How Radio Works

6.2 Receiving

" *No man would listen to you talk if he didn't know it was his turn next. – Edgar Watson Howe*

You can have your turn any time you want. But for now I hope you will continue receiving. The second half of radio communication story is just as spellbinding as the first half! Again we will examine AM first, followed by FM receiving. Let's see how things are going following transmission…

AM and SSB Receiving: When we last left our hero, *Audio Band*, he was trapped and hopelessly entangled within AM waveforms of radio frequencies being hurdled through space at the speed of light with no particular destination known! Is all hope lost for our hero? Will Audio Band ever again be free to vibrate the molecules of air as audible sound? Is there any chance he will be received and freed through the incredible power of demodulation?

But of course! It's *Superheterodyne* to the rescue!

Frequency Mixing: We interrupt this story to bring you the following hot background information that will help you comprehend the incredible demodulation power of Superheterodyne. The Superheterodyne receiver is well practiced in the art of *frequency mixing*, allowing it to convert high frequency radio signals into lower frequency signals while preserving any enveloping modulating signal, such as Audio Band! With this power, Superheterodyne may free Audio Band from his RF bondage!

When two signals of different frequencies are combined, or mixed, a lower frequency product signal results. (A higher frequency product also results that we will disregard, or filter away.) If one of the mixed frequencies contains modulation information, such as a modulating envelope of audio signals, that envelope of modulation will still shape the amplitude of the lower frequency product signal. That is, the amplitude modulation information is preserved. A component called **a mixer is used to convert a radio signal from one frequency to another.** [Visit the *HamRadioSchool.com* Section 6.2 learning media to find out more about frequency mixing.]

T7A03

Superheterodyne: The superheterodyne is just a fancy way of referring to a receiver that uses frequency mixing to begin extracting Audio Band from his RF prison. A superheterodyne receiver uses a mixer to shift the incoming signal to an intermediate frequency. That is, the received RF signal is mixed with another unmodulated RF signal of a different frequency, and a considerably lower frequency, still-modulated, RF signal results. We call this lower RF frequency the *intermediate frequency* (IF) because it is in between the originally received higher RF frequency and the much lower audio frequency that remains trapped in the modulating envelope of the IF signal.

More than one mixing stage may be used by a receiver to convert the modulated signal to lower frequencies. Once the modulated signal is converted low enough, the enveloping audio band signals may be extracted from it by electronic filtering. Figure 6.9 is a block diagram of a single-conversion superheterodyne receiver. It is a superheterodyne because it uses a mixer circuit to produce an intermediate frequency (IF) for the IF amplifier. It is a single-conversion type because it uses only one intermediate frequency step and, thus, it has only one IF amplifier.

Figure 6.10 is an elaborated version of Figure 6.9 illustrating the sequence of signal demodulation steps in a superheterodyne receiver. Follow along...

1. The modulated RF signal is mixed with the oscillator frequency.

2. The mixer produces the intermediate frequency with audio modulation information preserved in the IF signals.

3. The IF signals are amplified and sent to another mixing circuit (product detector).

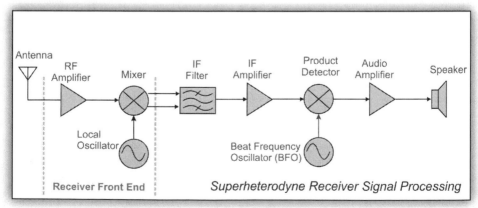

Figure 6.9: Single-Conversion Superheterodyne Block Diagram

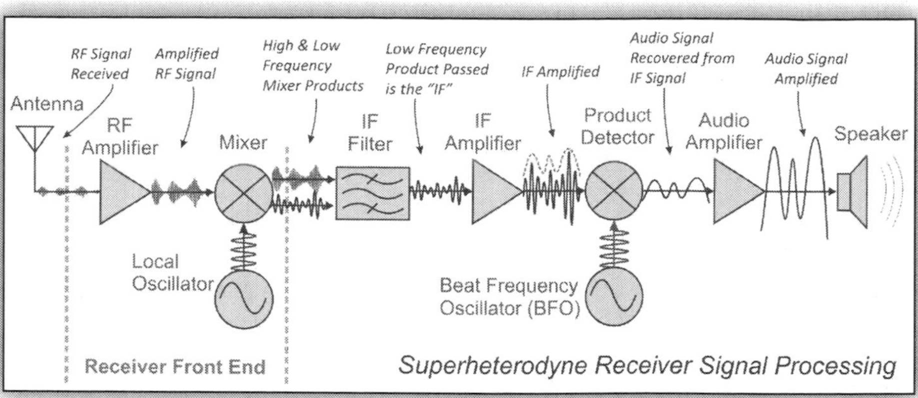

Figure 6.10: Superheterodyne Signal Demodulation Sequence

4. Mixing with the Beat Frequency Oscillator signal results in an even lower output frequency in the audio frequency range, allowing the preserved original audio band signal to be output to an audio amplifier.

5. The audio band signals are sent to a speaker where they are transformed into the original sound of your voice.

Voila! Audio Band is freed from his RF chains to grace the ears of another operator with the sound of your voice! With that big picture in mind, let's take a bit closer look at some receiver components and their functions.

RF Preamplifier: In many receivers **an RF preamplifier will be installed between the antenna and receiver** to boost weak RF signals before any mixing or demodulation is accomplished. This helps provide the mixer with stronger initial RF signals.

T7A11

Product Detector: The second mixer in the path of Figure 6.11 is referred to as the *product detector* because it begins the process of identifying audio signal products that are encoded in the IF signals (the modulation envelope information). The function of a product detector is to detect CW and SSB signals, and to begin the conversion of IF signals to lower frequencies for audio demodulation. **The ability of a receiver to detect the presence of a signal is called *sensitivity*.** The product detector's output results from mixing the IF with an unmodulated signal from the beat frequency oscillator.

T7A01

Oscillator: In Figure 6.10 two oscillator blocks are depicted in the processing path. The first oscillator provides the first mixer circuit an unmodulated

RF frequency to mix with a received RF signal to produce the intermediate frequency (IF) signal. This first oscillator in the path is a variable one, able to produce a wide range of frequencies for mixing with the received signal.

The ability to vary its mixing frequency is a very important function of this oscillator. And this oscillator is connected to your radio's tuning knob. This is the *variable frequency oscillator* (VFO) that you learned about in Section 1.1. When you tune your radio, this oscillator's frequency is adjusted so that it provides exactly the right mixing frequency to produce a single, constant IF value as the output of the mixer. The IF value always remains the same, and the VFO becomes a means of selecting the desired receive frequency from among all the various signals resonating on the antenna.

For instance, suppose you want to demodulate a 28.400 MHz signal as in our previous transmission example. The VFO is adjusted to provide a mixing frequency that combines with 28.400 MHz (and its RF band containing your voice signals) to produce the very specific IF for which the receiver has been specially designed to further process into audio frequencies. The frequency of 455 kHz (0.455 MHz) is a commonly used IF. All the other RF frequencies input from the antenna are also mixed with the VFO frequency and produce a variety of lower output frequencies, but only the specially selected IF signal of 455 kHz is processed beyond the mixer. All those other undesired mixer products are ignored and filtered away.

If you shift the VFO frequency to another value, the exact same IF (455 kHz) will result from VFO signal mixing with a different received frequency. So, in effect, the VFO allows you to select the received RF signals from your antenna that you wish to have mixed down to the IF value. This is how you tune your receiver to various selected frequencies.

Beat Frequency Oscillator: The second oscillator in the path, the *beat frequency oscillator* (BFO), serves a similar mixing function in a lower frequency range. It provides a mixing frequency to create even lower frequencies from the IF amplifier signals. These low products are the audio frequency envelope signals that feed the speaker and reproduce the sound of a transmitted voice.

RIT / Clarifier: The BFO may also be varied somewhat using a receiver control called **RIT (Receiver Incremental Tuning),** also known as the *clarifier*. By tweaking the BFO mixing frequency the demodulated audio signals can be adjusted slightly in sound frequency alignment. Every transceiver in the world is not calibrated perfectly, and sometimes the receiver's signal processing will not be aligned quite right with the proper audio output frequencies, even

T4B07

though your receiver display indicates that you are perfectly tuned to the carrier value.

For instance, the entire audio band may be processed a couple of hundred hertz high, making all the audio signals produce sound frequencies 200 Hz higher than the original voice frequencies. The received voice will sound artificially high pitched, perhaps a bit like Mickey Mouse! The RIT control allows you to vary the BFO slightly to adjust only the receiver's late stage processing and ratchet down those frequencies by 200 Hz to where the voice will sound correctly pitched. **The receiver incremental tuning, or receiver RIT is the control to use if the voice pitch of a single-sideband signal seems too high or too low.**

Note, with RIT only the receiver is adjusted, leaving the transmitter frequency to remain unchanged – you don't want to vary your transmitted frequency as your contact is dialing in your signal. If you try to correct the received pitch by retuning the transceiver (including transmission frequency), the two of you will chase each other around the dial trying to get your respective sound corrected! Use the RIT / clarifier, and leave your transmitter on one frequency.

Automatic Gain Control (AGC): Used to keep received audio relatively constant, the AGC in a superheterodyne receiver is a kind of feedback circuit. The AGC measures the output of the IF amplifier and adjusts the gain of preceding processing stages. As a result, the output amplitude of each signal processing stage is kept within the designed input range of the subsequent stage, avoiding distortion due to over-driving amplifiers or other circuits.

FM Receiving: Demodulating FM signals uses somewhat different techniques than the AM and SSB case, and there are several different varieties of FM demodulators. Demodulators are electronic circuits designed to evaluate the frequency deviations of the FM carrier and output signals with voltage variations that represent the frequency deviations. These voltage varied signals contain the original audio band information and drive the receiver's speaker to produce sound.

Take a look at Figure 6.11 on the next page and follow the path of FM receiver blocks. Like AM and SSB receiving, FM receivers will commonly use a preamplifier to boost RF signals right after the antenna. A mixer circuit with oscillator is followed by specially tuned filters to produce an intermediate frequency

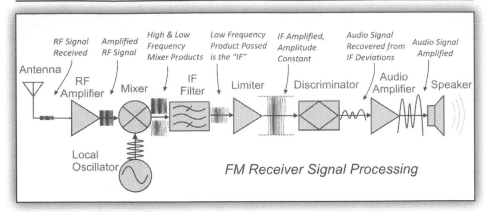

Figure 6.11: The FM receiver signal processing begins the same as the SSB superheterodyne, but a limiter circuit ensures a constant IF amplitude and a discriminator circuit recovers the audio signal from the IF deviations.

that is then amplified. The significant differences in the signal processing path from AM and SSB demodulation then follow.

Limiter: The *limiter* is a circuit that limits the amplitude of the FM signals going into the next stage demodulator circuit. The FM demodulator stage works best with a constant amplitude level, so the limiter helps keep the amplitude smoothed to a consistent level. Remember, the modulated voice information is contained in the frequency deviations, so limiting the amplitude of the signal does not impact the modulated information.

Discriminator: A *frequency discriminator* is one common type of FM demodulation circuit. A discriminator demodulates FM signals, extracting the audio signals from the frequency deviations. Only FM receivers have a discriminator. The discriminator evaluates the intermediate frequency deviations from resting state and translates them into variable amplitude audio signals for the speaker. Once again, your voice is decoded from a modulated RF signal and reproduced for the receiving radio operator!

Get to the questions on Receiving, *Section 6.2*. Next up we will compare bandwidth used by the various modes of transmission, along with a closer look at those "sidebands."

www.HamRadioSchool.com/tech_media

How Radio Works

6.3 **Bandwidth and Sidebands**

> **I'd really love to take that on, but I just don't have the bandwidth right now. — The Engineer's Excuse**

With all of the transmitting and receiving concepts under your belt you should now have the bandwidth to discuss a few very practical considerations regarding the small RF bands that are transmitted and received by your radio.

Bandwidth: Bandwidth implies capacity. In radio the bandwidth of a signal is the amount of spectrum used. Generally, the more bandwidth available the more information can be communicated per unit of time. With greater bandwidth of signals you can squeeze in more audio information and produce a higher quality sound. With narrow bandwidth the quality of sound may suffer, and the amount of information transmitted per unit of time is reduced. Each mode uses a unique amount of bandwidth. Let's see how they match up!

AM vs. SSB: We noted in an earlier section that **single sideband mode is a form of amplitude modulation,** or AM. We also noted that its primary advantage for voice transmission was its narrow bandwidth.

T8A01

As we have seen, voice modulation requires a band of radio frequencies to carry the information of the audio band signals produced by the microphone from your voice. In our example we considered a band of about 3,000 frequencies, or a bandwidth of about 3.0 kHz (3,000 Hz). **That is the approximate bandwidth of a single sideband voice signal: 3 kHz.** But why is it called "single sideband," and how does it compare with those other voice modes like AM and FM, or with CW?

T8A08

In Section 6.1 we introduced the concept that a true AM signal is redundant, producing two RF bands – one above the carrier frequency and a second below the carrier frequency. Figure 6.12 compares AM to SSB with frequency domain views. The upper band, or upper sideband (USB), is assigned by the transmitter by adding the audio frequency values to the carrier frequency,

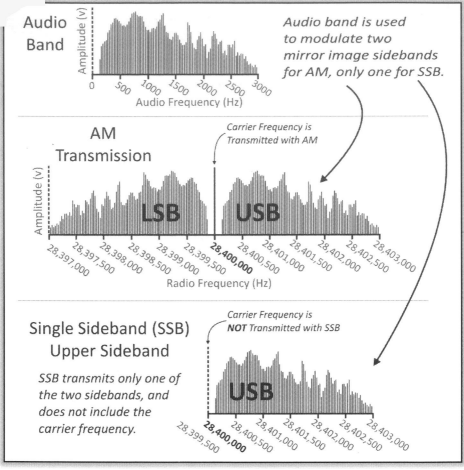

Audio Band — Amplitude (v) / Audio Frequency (Hz)

Audio band is used to modulate two mirror image sidebands for AM, only one for SSB.

AM Transmission — Amplitude (v) / Radio Frequency (Hz)

Carrier Frequency is Transmitted with AM

LSB   USB

Single Sideband (SSB) Upper Sideband

Carrier Frequency is **NOT** Transmitted with SSB

SSB transmits only one of the two sidebands, and does not include the carrier frequency.

USB

Figure 6.12: AM and Single Sideband Comparison

just as in the example of Section 6.1. The lower sideband (LSB) is assigned by subtracting the audio frequency values from the carrier frequency value.

Both sidebands carry the exact same information, a redundant encoding of the voice audio band. The two sidebands are like mirror images of one another. This redundancy provides AM with a robust signal and improved reliability, but it consumes a lot of bandwidth, approximately 6 kHz, or about twice that used by SSB.

SSB mode uses only one of the two AM sidebands, and it does not transmit the central carrier frequency. So, SSB is truly a single sideband. Your receiver artificially reproduces the carrier frequency as a reference point so that all the individual sideband frequencies may be recovered.

Which sideband does your radio use, upper or lower? The answer is, "it depends!" The standard worldwide agreed convention for SSB voice is to use upper sideband for bands 30m and higher frequency. So, **the upper sideband is normally used for 10 meter HF, VHF, and UHF single sideband communications.** The lower sideband is normally used in the lower frequency bands of HF for SSB phone (40m through 160m bands).

T8A06

FM Bandwidth: Recall that FM bandwidth changes with the amplitude of the audio signal driving the frequency deviations. Louder sound means greater audio signal power (greater amplitude) that is converted into greater frequency deviations in the FM transmitted RF band. **FM phone bandwidth, such as a VHF repeater signal, is typically between 10 and 15 kHz.** So, FM requires up to five times the bandwidth of SSB, but it offers the advantages of clear, robust audio.

T8A09

CW Bandwidth: CW is the type of emission that has the narrowest bandwidth. Since CW is transmitting only a single carrier wave for tone production, **the maximum bandwidth required to transmit is very narrow, typically around 150 Hz.** That's only 5% of SSB bandwidth!

T8A05 T8A11

With CW and many digital modes that use narrow bandwidth, low power operation (QRP) is very popular. Long distance contacts can be made on just a few watts of power since the transmitted power is condensed into the very narrow band of frequencies, not spread out over thousands of hertz of frequencies as in phone modes. You can get a lot of signal 'punch' with CW!

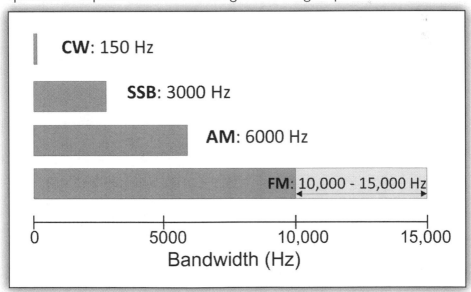

Figure 6.13: Comparison of Approximate Bandwidths by Mode

Edge of Band Considerations: Look back to Section 4.2 at the FCC amateur band plan that defines the limits of Technician license privileges. Obviously there are edges to the bands where your technician privileges will end. You are not allowed to transmit beyond those edge limits with even a single hertz in your small transmitted band of RF frequencies! Take note...

Transmitter frequency displays have calibration error that you must allow for.

Transmitter frequency can drift over time.

Your modulation sidebands must not extend beyond the band edge.

For all these reasons you should not set your transmit frequency to be exactly at the edge of an amateur band or sub-band.

For example: Suppose you are operating on 10m phone, properly using the upper sideband (USB). What is the highest frequency that you should tune to so that you avoid transmitting outside of your Technician privileges?

Examine Figure 6.14. The Technician 10m phone privileges extend up to 28.500 MHz. Your USB signal is about 3 kHz wide, extending above your tuned carrier frequency shown on the radio display. At the very least you should not transmit when tuned above a frequency 3 kHz below 28.500 MHz.

28.500 MHz – 0.003 MHz = 28.497 MHz   (3 kHz = 0.003 MHz)

So you should not transmit in SSB mode above 28.497 MHz because your 3 kHz bandwidth USB signal may extend above the Technician limit of 28.500 MHz. But keep in mind the drift and calibration error as well.

It may be prudent to cut that maximum by another few hertz, just to be sure! Maybe 28.496.500 MHz max, giving you a 500 Hz buffer for drift and calibration error.

Transverters: A transverter allows you to extend your radio's capabilities into higher RF bands. It converts a transmitter's modulated emissions into modulated frequencies of a higher band altogether. For example, **a transverter could take the output of a low-powered 28 MHz SSB exciter** (the signal from your transceiver) **and produce a 222 MHz output signal,** retaining the modulated information across the frequency conversion. If you

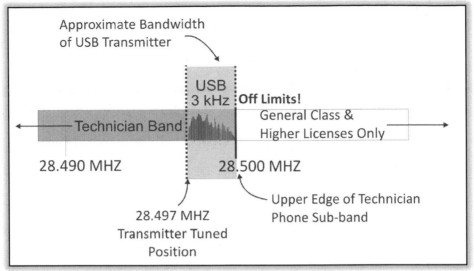

Figure 6.14: Edge of Band Tuning Considerations for Bandwidth

should get into transverting, perhaps to transmit in the microwave frequency bands allocated to amateur use, take great care to ensure your transmissions remain within the privileges of your license.

Whew! Take a deep series of breaths. Congratulations! You made it through some of the most challenging material of this book. If you didn't quite get it all, don't worry. You will over time, as your amateur radio bandwidth expands, and even if some of your understanding comes after you've got your Technician license hanging in your ham shack. Zero-in on those highlighted test question topics and reread this chapter's three sections a little at a time. Check out the web site for additional materials about the workings of radio. You'll be glad you did!

And while you're at it now, keep the book handy and go work through the questions for **Section 6.3**. You're on your way to really getting it!

www.HamRadioSchool.com/tech_media

Note: *FM bandwidth in the amateur radio practice is commonly greater than the 10 to 15 kHz range stated in the exam question pool material and in this section. You may experience bandwidths closer to 10 to 20 kHz in practice.*

Beautiful antenna farm of Frank, K7SFN, overlooking
snowy Nevada mountains.   *Photo courtesy of K7SFN*

7.0   Antennas

The o
ch

> **‟** *Invisible airwaves crackle with life*
> *Bright antennae bristle with the energy*
>   *— The Spirit of Radio, Neil Peart [Rush]*

Nothing inspires awe, appreciation, and fun projects among hams more than a well-crafted, highly effective antenna! There is just something about gleaming aluminum and copper, wire and welds, connectors and coax all coming together to bristle with the energy and radiate information across the vast landscape. It's a fact: Antennas are fascinating and very cool.

Antennas are sort of like the filaments of light bulbs! They receive electrical energy and radiate much of it as electromagnetic energy. Where a light bulb filament radiates visible light EM (and a fair amount of infrared heat), your radio antenna radiates radio frequency EM. But unlike the light bulb your antenna's EM emissions may be detected around the world!

In this chapter we will start with some basics about antenna characteristics and designs. In Section 7.2 we will learn about standing wave ratio (SWR) and how to get the most out of your antenna system. Section 7.3 wraps up the antenna admiration with practical considerations about coaxial cable and connectors.

7.1   Antennas
Antenna Basics

Resonance: Antennas radiate best when they resonate with the frequency of transmission. Think of pushing someone on a swing, where you can time your pushes so that the swing continues to go back and forth with only a slight reinforcing shove each back-and-forth cycle. The oscillating period of the swing and your timed pushes are in resonance with one another, and you can keep the swing going very efficiently with little effort.

cillating period of the swing is determined by the length of the rope or ain by which it hangs – a long rope produces a long period back-and-forth, while a short rope results in quick back-and-forth. The period of an antenna's oscillation, or its resonant frequency, is determined largely by the antenna's physical length. The timing of the pushes the antenna gets is determined by the radio frequency fed into it by the transmitter.

So an antenna should be trimmed to the proper resonant length for the frequency it is intended to radiate in order for it to radiate efficiently and not waste your transmitter's energy to heat.

Lower frequency bands where wavelengths are long will need a longer antenna. High frequencies with short wavelengths resonate with shorter antennas. You can change the resonant frequency of an antenna by lengthening or shortening its conductive element. **For instance, to change a dipole antenna to make it resonate on a higher frequency, you would shorten it.** (See dipole antenna type later in this section.)

The resonant length of an antenna is a multiple of the wavelength it is intended to radiate, and fractional multiples such as ½ or ¼ wavelength are very common. In general, longer antennas such as ½ wavelength provide very good performance, while antennas of less than ¼ wavelength (like that short rubber duck on an HT) will be less effective radiators of RF.

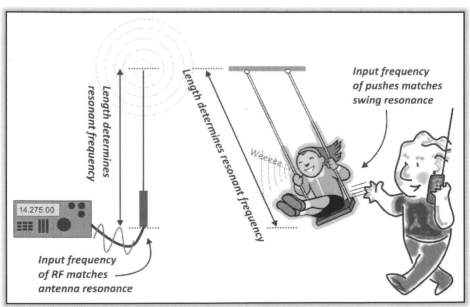

Figure 7.1: Concept of Resonance

Antenna Types: The names of basic antenna types tend to tell a lot about the antenna. Usually the name has been derived from the physical form, the orientation, the length, or the effects of the antenna type. Here are some relevant examples.

Vertical Antenna: A simple antenna oriented vertically to the earth's surface. Regarding the EM field polarization, **a vertical antenna produces an electric field that is perpendicular to the earth** as well.

T9A02

Quarter Wave Vertical: A commonly used vertical antenna is the ¼ wave vertical, meaning its height is ¼ of its resonant frequency wavelength. As you can easily calculate, a ¼ wave antenna for the 2 meter band will extend approximately 2m x 0.25 = 0.5m, or about 1.5 feet. A ¼ wave vertical for the 40m band would stand about 10m high, or about 30 feet. We'll get into calculating antenna lengths more a bit later in this section.

Ground Plane: A ¼ wave vertical works best when it has a ground plane. A ground plane is a conductive surface perpendicular to the antenna that acts like a mirror for RF purposes. A car's metal rooftop can serve as a very effective ground plane for a VHF or UHF ¼ wave vertical antenna. The ground plane's RF mirror essentially creates another virtual ¼ wave antenna as a mirror image of the real ¼ wave vertical, and electrically the real and virtual antennas complement one another to act much like a longer and more efficient ½ wave antenna. Way cool, huh?

A collection of radially oriented wires extending from the base of a ground mounted vertical may serve as a ground plane, and

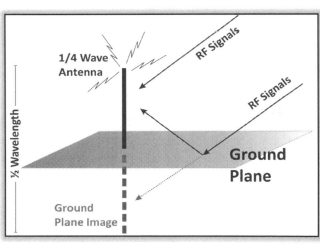

Figure 7.2: 1/4 Wave Antenna Ground Plane

some antennas will have abbreviated ground planes made from three or four short radials angled down slightly from the base of a vertical. For an indoor VHF or UHF antenna, mounting it on a metal cookie sheet or a plane of aluminum foil can really improve performance.

Dipole Antenna: The dipole is another simple antenna. You may think of the dipole as two ¼ wave antennas placed end-to-end, almost like having the virtual ground plane image of a ¼ wave antenna turned physically real. A dipole is typically ½ wavelength long, with two conductors (frequently copper wires) extending in opposite directions. One of the conductors is attached to the RF conducting side of the feedline from the transceiver, such as the center wire conductor of a coaxial cable. The other conductor is attached to the ground side of the feedline, such as the braided shield portion of a coax cable.

A half-wave wire dipole is a common and inexpensive way to radiate the long wavelengths of the HF bands. For erecting convenience, a lengthy wire **simple dipole is most often mounted parallel to the earth's surface, and thus is a horizontally polarized antenna.** The dipole is also said to be a *center fed antenna* because the feedline from the transceiver attaches at the center point and each of the conductors is of equivalent length.

T9A03

Radiating Pattern: A half-wave dipole antenna in free space radiates strongest broadside to the antenna. In other words, the strongest RF emissions come out radially away from the dipole's conductors, or wires. The radiating strength pattern looks a bit like a big donut with the wire running

T9A10

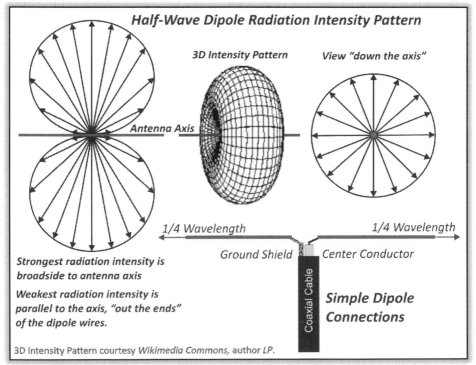

Figure 7.3: Dipole Antenna Radiating Pattern in Free Space

right through the donut hole. The poorest RF emissions are directly out the ends of the dipole's wires.

RF Coupling: The *free space* part of the previous highlighted statement means the dipole has no objects nearby it and it is far above the ground – in each case, at least several wavelengths worth of space. (The perfect model dipole has infinite space around it, but of course that is just a model.) The reason this is important is because of an effect called *RF coupling*. Radiating antennas are affected by surrounding conductors, such as metal and the ground. The antenna's pattern of radiation, and its resonant frequency, can be significantly altered by surrounding conductors and by its height above the ground.

Beam or Directional Antennas: Beam antennas are designed to concentrate signals in one direction. The physical design of beam antennas is more complex than verticals or dipoles, and many types of beam antennas will have multiple elements (active and passive conductor components) to take advantage of the effects of RF coupling to shape the radiating pattern. **Examples of directional antennas include the quad, Yagi, and dish** antenna types. `T9A01` `T9A06`

Antenna Gain: Directional or beam antennas are said to have gain in the direction of the concentrated signals. **Gain means that the antenna produces increased signal strength in a specific direction when compared to a reference antenna.** The theoretical free space dipole discussed earlier is a common standard reference for comparison, as is the isotropic (radiating evenly in all directions) vertical antenna. `T9A11`

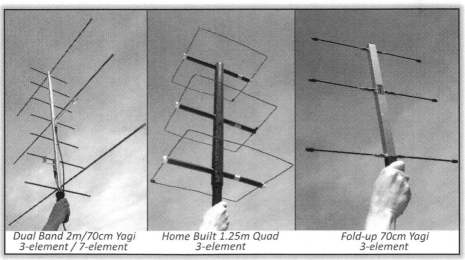

Dual Band 2m/70cm Yagi 3-element / 7-element	Home Built 1.25m Quad 3-element	Fold-up 70cm Yagi 3-element

Figure 7.4: Three Different VHF/UHF Directional Antennas

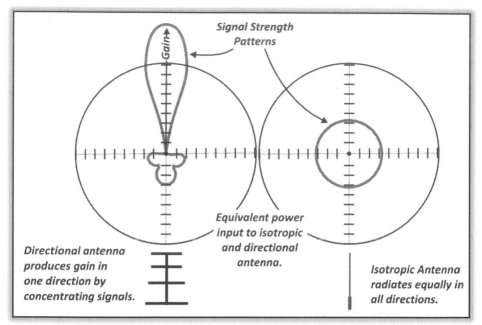

Figure 7.5: Gain Pattern of a Directional Antenna

Think about gain this way: The reference antenna spreads the power of the transmitter evenly in all directions, more or less. Imagine you use an RF field strength meter to measure the transmitted electric field strength 100 feet away from the antenna. Suppose you get a reading of 1.0 in this case. (Just a relative measure; we'll discuss units of RF field strength later.) Then you switch to a beam antenna and measure in the direction of concentrated emissions, again 100 feet away from the antenna. This time your field strength meter reads 6.0.

In the direction of the beam your antenna is providing signal gain of a 6:1 ratio. However, if you measure behind the beam or to the side, you will find the RF field strength to be less than that of the reference antenna, perhaps a reading of 0.1 or less. All of the energy that the isotropic reference antenna spread around has been pointed in one direction to provide gain. Essentially,, the evenly distributed isotropic signal that works equally well in all directions has been traded for much improved performance in one direction. With antennas, everything is a trade-off.

Dummy Load: A *dummy load* is not an antenna. Rather, it is a non-emitting substitute for an antenna. From the transmitter's electrical point of view the dummy load looks like an antenna, but it merely dissipates the transmitted energy into heat instead of radiating RF energy. **The purpose of a dummy load is to prevent the radiation of signals when making tests** of your transmitter. A dummy load may be a small, ceramic module for low power use, or a large can of mineral oil with an antenna connector integrated onto it for very high power absorption. Technically speaking, **a dummy load consists of a non-inductive resistor and a heat sink,** which means that in use it does not create undesirable electronic effects and it can dissipate the heat generated by the RF. (Resistors and inductance topics coming in Chapter 9.)

Antenna Length: The actual length of an antenna's conducting element is usually slightly less than its wavelength multiple due to some complex electrical dynamics of finite length radiating element. Still, a close approximation of ideal antenna length can be calculated with simple formulas.

To calculate approximate antenna length in meters, multiply the resonant frequency's wavelength by the antenna multiple (1/4 wave, 1/2 wave, etc.) as illustrated earlier in this section. To calculate approximate antenna length in feet or inches, use the following formulas:

> For ½ Wavelength Antennas
> > 468 ÷ frequency in MHz = Length in Feet

> For ¼ Wavelength Antennas
> > 234 ÷ frequency in MHz = Length in Feet

> To convert to inches, multiply Length in Feet x 12.

Example 1: **Approximate length, in inches, of a quarter-wavelength vertical antenna for 146 MHz is...**

> **234 ÷ 146 = 1.60 feet;**
> **1.60 x 12 = 19 inches**

The approximate length is 19 inches.

Example 2: **Approximate length, in inches, of a 6 meter ½-wavelength wire dipole antenna is...**

> **468 ÷ 50 = 9.36 feet (Note: 6m frequency is 50 MHz)**
> **9.63 x 12 = 112 inches**

The approximate length is 112 inches. Notice in this example that it was first necessary to convert 6m into its commensurate frequency of 50 MHz. Remember from Section 4.1, Wavelength & Frequency:

T7C13

T9A08

T9A09

300 ÷ wavelength = frequency in MHz
So, 300 ÷ 6 = 50 MHz

The values 468 and 234 come from conversions between the use of feet and the use of meters for wavelength measurement, plus a 5% length adjustment. Notice that the ¼ wavelength dividend, 234, is exactly one-half the ½ wavelength dividend, 468. It is easy to remember that these numbers are sequential counting numbers (2, 3, 4) and sequential even numbers (4, 6, 8).

Mobile Antennas: Antennas used with mobile stations, such as in motor vehicles, require a little special consideration due to the unique requirements of a mobile station. For instance, mobile antenna length is limited by safety practicality, and a mobile station does not have a static environment from which it transmits consistently.

T9A13 **Mobile antennas are often mounted in the center of the vehicle roof because that normally provides the most uniform radiation pattern.** The flat roof acts as a ground plane for the vertical antenna, and an uneven ground plane results in uneven performance patterns for the antenna. Still, good (if uneven) antenna performance can result from other mounting positions on a vehicle.

The radiation pattern of a vertical antenna is also affected by the antenna length, and a greater variety of vertical antenna lengths is available beyond the common 1/4 and 1/2 wavelength discussed earlier in this section. **For** **T9A12** **VHF or UHF mobile service a properly mounted 5/8 wavelength antenna will offer a lower angle of radiation and more gain than a 1/4 wavelength antenna, usually providing improved coverage.** The improved gain of the 5/8 wavelength antenna comes from concentrating the signals more horizontally than the 1/4 wavelength antenna. So, if you wish to operate in areas where VHF or UHF repeaters are at high angles to your traveling routes, such as below nearby mountaintop or skyscraper positioned repeaters, the higher radiation angles of the 1/4 wave antenna may provide better performance. Remember, every antenna is a trade-off.

Loading: Because mobile antennas cannot be physically long enough to be at least 1/4 wavelength radiators for most of the long-wavelength HF bands (10 to 160 meter bands), electronic tricks are used to make shorter antennas behave like longer antennas. These tricks are called *loading* the antenna, and loading makes the antenna seem electrically longer than it is physically. So, a relatively short antenna on a vehicle can be made to radiate frequencies much lower than its physical length allows in the non-loaded case.

One common loading method is to insert a conductive coil into the antenna. These coils are called *inductors*, and they impact the flow of AC in the antenna. We will explore the effects of inductors more in Chapter 8, but **one type of loading when referring to an antenna is inserting an inductor in the radiating portion of the antenna to make it electrically longer.**

T9A14

An inductor may also be used along with other loading components, such as a *capacitor, or capacitance hat.* This may be a disk or spoked ring added to the antenna's radiating element, and it can further enhance the low frequency radiating ability of a physically short antenna, helping the antenna circuit to resonate at the lower frequencies.

Photo: Paul, AAØK
High-Q-Antennas

What's the trade-off with loaded antennas? Most full-sized antennas will radiate very effectively across a wide range of frequency values either side of the specific frequency for which its length is cut. So, you can use one antenna length to get good performance across the entire 20-meter band, for instance, a bandwidth of over 300 kHz. However, as you load an antenna and physically shorten it, the range of frequencies over which the antenna radiates efficiently becomes narrower. A physically short, highly loaded 20-meter antenna may perform well over only 100 kHz or less, depending on the amount of loading.

Figure 7.6: An inductor loaded mobile antenna.

Don't run out to make invisible airwaves crackle with life just yet! There's more to know about antennas, about confirming resonant performance, and about feedlines and connectors. Read on, but first try the online questions for **Section 7.1** and make sure you've really got it!

www.HamRadioSchool.com/tech_media

Photo: Joyce, KØJJW

Bob, KØNR, readies a 6m Yagi directional for VHF contesting.

Antennas

7.2 **Standing Wave Ratio (SWR)**

" *An antenna is just an electromagnetic fishing pole. – Anonymous Ham*

Once you have an approximate length for your antenna element you may want to trim its length more precisely in order to achieve the best resonance performance feasible. You'll catch more RF fish that way.

You can gauge your antenna's proper trim length by measuring how well it resonates across the frequencies of the band for which it is designed. By trimming the length you can alter the resonant frequency for the antenna to be higher or lower in the band. One way to gauge the resonant frequency in an antenna system is by evaluating the *standing wave ratio*, or SWR.

Standing Wave Ratio (SWR)

SWR: SWR is the ratio of the electrical voltage in the forward direction to your antenna with the electrical voltage of reflections in the reverse direction back toward the transmitter. This ratio of forward and reverse voltages indicates how well your antenna, feedline, and transmitter are electrically *matched* with one another. Voltage levels directly impact the power directed into an antenna system, and electrical mismatches create power reflections in the system. Optimally, all electrical power sent forward to the antenna will be radiated and zero power will be reflected, but such perfection is rarely achieved in an antenna system. Although SWR is a voltage ratio, it is most often calculated from measurements of power in each direction.

SWR may be calculated like this: $\mathrm{SWR} = \dfrac{\sqrt{\mathrm{Fwd\ Pwr}} + \sqrt{\mathrm{Refl\ Pwr}}}{\sqrt{\mathrm{Fwd\ Pwr}} - \sqrt{\mathrm{Refl\ Pwr}}}$

Notice in this calculation that the very best condition, where all power is moving forward toward the antenna and zero power is reflected back, results in a 1/1 voltage ratio, or 1:1. As reflected power increases, the ratio begins to increase. For instance, imagine you measured in your transmission line a forward power of 81 watts and a reflected power of 9 watts. The SWR would be 2:1, calculated like this:

$$SWR = \frac{\sqrt{81}+\sqrt{9}}{\sqrt{81}-\sqrt{9}} = \frac{9+3}{9-3} = \frac{12}{6} = \frac{2}{1} \text{ or } 2:1$$

You can see from these calculations that a low SWR ratio like 1:1 is very good, meaning that little power is reflecting back from your antenna. And a high SWR ratio, say 4:1, is poor because it means quite a lot of transmitter power is being reflected back from the antenna instead of being radiated. Much of that power is being wasted.

In general terms, **SWR is a measure of how well a load is matched to a transmission line.** In most cases the load is an antenna. The word "matched" in this definition means *impedance* match.

Impedance: Impedance is a measure of the opposition to the flow of an alternating current (AC) in a circuit. You may think of it like resistance to the flow of electrons back and forth in the wires. (We'll cover this more in Section 8.1, *Electric Basics*.) **The unit of impedance is the Ohm.**

Impedance Matching: In antennas and antenna feedlines, it is important to ensure that impedance is matched, or the same, throughout the system from the transceiver to the antenna. The antenna, the feedline, and the transmitter should all have equivalent characteristic impedance. When the system is matched like this, the reflected power will be minimized and the antenna radiation will be greatest. The antenna resonant frequency, in large part determined by antenna length, is one factor affecting an antenna's impedance.

Impedance Mismatch: If the components of your antenna system are not impedance matched, power will be reflected where impedance changes exist, and SWR will rise. This may occur due to any of the following reasons:
- Improperly trimmed antenna length for frequency
- Different, unmatched impedance feedline segments or connectors
- Loose antenna or feedline connectors
- Open or shorted feedline or antenna conductors
- Moisture in a coaxial cable feedline
- Metal conductors near the antenna affecting impedance
- Antenna height above ground insufficient
- Other factors

50 Ohm Impedance: Most modern amateur radios are engineered to use 50 Ohm impedance coaxial cable and connectors. **The impedance of the most commonly used coaxial cables in typical amateur radio installations is 50 Ohms.**

Antenna Tuner: An antenna tuner matches the antenna system impedance to the transceiver's output impedance. This device, common with HF transceivers, uses electronic networks to artificially adjust the apparent impedance of the antenna system (feedline, connectors, and antenna) as "sensed" by the transceiver.

An antenna tuner can help boost the power sent to a poorly matched antenna system because most modern transceivers will automatically begin to reduce output power as the antenna system impedance deviates from the designed value (usually 50 Ohms). While the tuner cannot actually change the impedance of the feedline and antenna, it can present the transceiver with an impedance near its designed value to avoid the automatic power reductions, and then safely handle the reflected power so it does not damage the transceiver. More power will be radiated by the antenna simply because the transceiver power reduction is avoided, but the impedance mismatch and associated power reflections are not completely eliminated by the tuner.

Measuring SWR: There are a couple of different ways to measure SWR in your antenna system. Usually you will position a measuring device between the transceiver and feedline, or connect a measurement device to your feedline without connecting to your transceiver. Usually an antenna and feedline system SWR is not measured with an antenna tuner in the circuit.

SWR Meter: An in-line SWR Power Meter connects in series with the feedline, between the transmitter and antenna. It will monitor the SWR by measuring forward and reflected power simultaneously. Usually a direct readout of SWR is provided. Frequently these meters will provide "cross needle readout" whereby forward power is indicated by one needle, reverse power by a second needle, and the crossing position of the two needles indicates SWR on a separately printed scale on the meter face. See Figure 7.7.

Directional Wattmeter: A directional wattmeter reads power in only one direction at a time, allowing for separate measurements of forward power and reflected power. A manual calculation of SWR may then be undertaken as described earlier in this section. **A directional wattmeter could be used to determine if a feedline and antenna are properly matched, if an SWR meter is not available.**

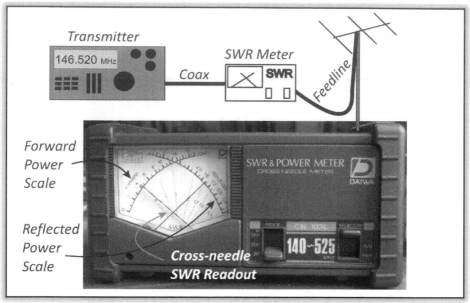

Figure 7.7: Typical Cross Needle SWR Meter and Connection

Antenna Analyzer: An antenna analyzer is an instrument that can be used to determine if an antenna is resonant at the desired operating frequency. The analyzer connects to the antenna system without the transceiver and sends variable frequency signals to the antenna system. These signals allow rapid measurement of SWR across a broad band of frequencies. Minimized SWR readings indicate resonant frequencies for the antenna system, and those frequencies are indicated on the analyzer display.

SWR Ratios: What SWR ratio should you expect from your antenna system? The ratio of 1:1 is best, as we've noted, since **a 1:1 reading on an SWR meter indicates a perfect impedance match between the antenna and the feedline,** and no reflections or loss of power. A well-constructed and well-trimmed antenna can usually achieve 1.5:1, or lower.

Here are some additional guidelines about SWR ratios:

2:1 is the approximate SWR value above which protection circuits in most solid-state transmitters begin to reduce transmitter power.

3:1 SWR is the value above which many antenna tuners will no longer be able to provide the transceiver a matching impedance.

4:1 SWR reading means an impedance mismatch.

Generally, you should strive for low SWR in your antenna system. Most VHF and UHF commercially manufactured antennas will have pre-set SWR trims that are well below 2:1, and further trimming is unwarranted. If you choose to construct your own antennas, a challenge that many hams love to take on, you will surely want to thoroughly check and trim your creations.

Most wire dipoles applied to HF operations will require trimming of length to achieve good SWR values, since an antenna's resonant frequency is one significant factor affecting its impedance. Depending on design and environmental circumstances, it may be desirable to tweak the trim of a wire dipole such that the minimum SWR is in the portion of the amateur band where your license privileges apply.

For example, because the 10 meter band is quite wide, extending for 1.7 MHz of bandwidth, it is sometimes difficult to maintain low SWR across the entire band of frequencies with a single dipole design. However, the Technician privileges are in the lowest 0.5 MHz (500 kHz) of the 10m band. So, you may wish to trim the length of your 10m dipole to minimize SWR near the lower part of the 10m band, perhaps with an optimum frequency near 28.300 MHz. That way, it is likely that a single dipole will provide good SWR across the 500 kHz of Technician frequencies.

SWR Curves: An SWR curve of your antenna system performance may be plotted as is Figure 7.8 on the next page. You may measure SWR with one of the instruments discussed in this section and plot the results of SWR across a band of frequencies. A typical SWR curve will be U-shaped or V-shaped, and it will move up or down the frequency spectrum as you trim, or make changes in the length of the dipole antenna. Generally, trimming the dipole shorter will move the SWR curve to the right and match your antenna to higher frequencies. Lengthening the dipole has the opposite effect, moving the curve to the left and matching the antenna to lower frequencies. By properly trimming your dipole antenna you may center the best SWR performance in the portion of the band where you expect to operate your station the most.

SWR Bandwidth: The range of frequencies for which an antenna provides a desired value of SWR or lower is referred to as the SWR bandwidth. For example, in the "Middle Antenna Trim" of Figure 7.8 the "2:1 SWR bandwidth" is indicated to be approximately 28.020 MHz to 28.560 MHz. That is the band for which the SWR is 2:1 or lower. This is a 2:1 SWR bandwidth of 540 kHz (0.540 MHz). Harkening back to the loaded antenna topic of Section 7.1, the

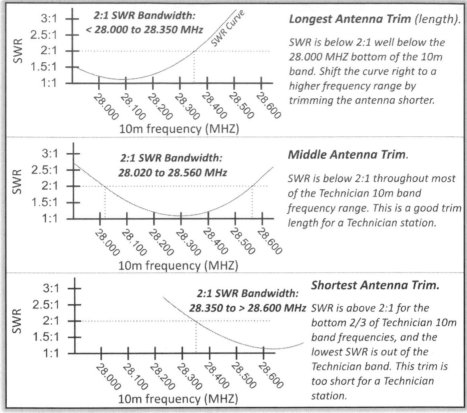

Figure 7.8: SWR Curves Changing with Antenna Trim Length

SWR bandwidth will become narrower as antenna loading is implemented to allow operation with substantially shortened antenna physical lengths.

Now you can make sure you are casting efficiently and effectively with your electromagnetic fishing poles. You won't have to worry about SWR adjustment with most purchased HT vertical antennas or rubber ducks, nor with most VHF and UHF mobile antennas used on your car or in your home. But soon, when you start creating your own gleaming lovelies or purchasing a commercial wire dipole, you'll want to make sure you've done your due diligence with trimming, and drive that SWR as low as possible in the frequency ranges you plan to use.

Good luck with those future endeavors and with the fishing, but study the questions for *Section 7.2* first!

www.HamRadioSchool.com/tech_media

7.3 Antennas
Coax and Connectors

ℓℓ *Many a live wire would be a dead one except for his connections. – Wilson Mizner*

The SWR of your antenna system is a vital consideration for effective RF emissions, especially with the use of coaxial cable. **It is important to have a low SWR in an antenna system that uses coaxial cable feed-line to allow the efficient transfer of power and reduce losses.** In this section we will take a close look at the characteristics of coaxial cable because it is very commonly used by amateur operators, and at the connectors that keep it live.

Coaxial Cable: Coaxial cable is commonly used to carry RF signals between radio and antenna. It is used more often than any other feedline for amateur radio antenna systems because it is easy to use and requires few special installation considerations.

Physical Features: Coaxial cable, or *coax*, has a center conductor (typically copper) that may be solid or multi-stranded wire. The center conductor is surrounded by a tubular dielectric insulator, such as a plastic like polyethylene. A metallic shield or braid surrounds the insulator and center conductor, helping to reduce RF interference. **The use of shielded wire prevents coupling of unwanted signals to or from the wire.** A plastic or rubber jacket forms the exterior of the coax, protecting against moisture penetration and helping maintain the integrity of the cable.

T9B01

T7C12 T9B03

T6D12

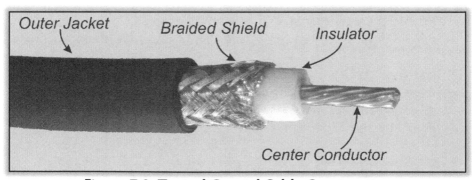

Figure 7.9: Typical Coaxial Cable Construction

Electrical Features: No RF feedline provides perfect, lossless transmission of power. Each type of coax has unique impedance and RF signal loss characteristics. These electrical features are affected by the physical dimensions of the cable and the type of materials used. The diameter of the cable and the type of dielectric insulation material are two of the more common physical features of interest that impact both impedance value and loss characteristics.

Skin Effect: Radio frequency signals tend to travel on the outside surface of conductors, including the center conductor of coaxial cable. Megahertz range RF electric signals with frequencies much higher than standard alternating household current (a mere 60 Hz) do not penetrate deeply into the conducting material. This is referred to as *skin effect.* Since the electromagnetic fields tend to flow near and around the skin of the wire conductor, the materials immediately surrounding the conductor affect the electrical signal transmission speed and the signal loss. The diameter of the conductor also has an effect, since more surface area provides less impedance to electron flow.

Feedline Loss: Power lost in a feedline is converted into heat. Generally, as the frequency of a signal passing through coaxial cable is increased the loss increases. Generally, electrical loss will be greater with narrower gauge coaxial cable and loss will be less with larger cable. **(Example: Larger diameter RG-8 coax has less loss for a given frequency than smaller RG-58 coax.) For VHF and UHF frequencies, air-insulated hard line has the lowest loss characteristics.** As the name implies, air insulated cable uses simply air between the center conductor wire and the surrounding shield.

Moisture Contamination is the most common cause for failure of coax cable.

1. Air core or air insulated coax requires special techniques to prevent water absorption, as compared to more common foam or solid dielectric types. Air core must be carefully sealed at connectors and other precautions taken, and **this is a disadvantage** of air core.

2. Ultraviolet light can damage the outer jacket material allowing water to enter the cable, so the outer jacket should be resistant to ultraviolet light. All types of coax can be damaged over time by the sun's ultraviolet rays.

3. Coax connectors exposed to the weather should be sealed against water intrusion to prevent increased feedline loss.

Connectors for coaxial cable have unique form factors and sizes that are intended for use with specific cable diameters and for various frequency applications.

PL-259 Connector is commonly used at HF frequencies. It imposes some significant signal loss at higher frequencies, particularly in the UHF range. Still, this is one of the most commonly used connectors for all applications. The female matching connector to the PL-259 is designated the SO-239 connector.

T9B07

Type N-Connector is most suitable for frequencies above 400 MHz. The N-connector is commonly used for UHF applications and many operators prefer their lower loss characteristics for VHF frequencies as well.

T9B06

SMA Connector is a small diameter coax connector that has become very popular for HT radio use in recent years. The SMA connector offers good performance at VHF and UHF frequencies.

Figure 7.10: Common Coaxial Cable Connector Types

BNC Connector is a common connector on HT radios, particularly older models. It is still widely used, it is a sturdy connector option for smaller diameter coax, and it offers good performance for VHF and UHF frequencies.

T9B09 **Care and Maintenance: A loose connection in an antenna or feed-line,** usually at a connector, **can cause erratic changes in SWR readings.** Carefully mount connectors to coax and properly solder the connections for both center conductor and shield. Seal connectors well if they will be exposed to the weather. Check the condition of your coax outer jacket for cracks, stiffness, or other indications that moisture may be able to penetrate.

Be aware that there are many different varieties of coaxial cable suitable for amateur radio use. The best cable to use often depends upon the specific application, the length of the cable run, and your budget. Before you design an antenna system for your ham shack, take some time to investigate the signal loss values and costs of various feedline options, as well as factors such as flexibility and power handling capacity.

Prefabricated coaxial cables can be purchased from vendors in lengths that you specify, or in standard precut lengths, and with or without connectors of your choosing attached and soldered into place. You may prefer to learn how to attach and solder connectors yourself, saving dollars and taking pride in a more hand-crafted system with which you will have familiarity for maintenance and repair purposes.

There are other types of feedlines with different characteristics. Flat twin lead cable and "ladder line" is quite popular and used for many applications. Twin lead offers no shielding like coax, so it is more susceptible to electronic and RF noise interference than coax, but its low loss electrical characteristics are very desirable for some types of antenna applications.

I hope that you can keep your radio's wires live with solid connections using what you've learned in this section. But before you run out to run cable to your bristling antenna farm, try the questions for *Section 7.3*. I think you'll find them rather easy now!

www.HamRadioSchool.com/tech_media

8.0   It's Electric!

❝ Electricity is really just organized lightning. – George Carlin

The little slivers of lightning within your radio are indeed highly organized, performing many precision tasks! Understanding of the organization and the nature of the radio's electrical tasks starts with the basic characteristics of organized lightning. Let's strike!

In this chapter we will first examine the basic characteristic of electricity in Section 8.1 and introduce a water flow model that will help us think about how electricity works. Voltage, current, resistance, and the units of measurement for each are simply defined and explained in terms that are almost exactly like water flowing in pipes.

In Section 8.2 we will learn two fundamental laws of electricity: Ohm's Law and the Power Law. These laws describe the basic behaviors of electricity. We will expand the water flow model and use some easy-to-remember tools for calculating electrical values with these laws. We will also introduce the decibel and describe how power relationships are defined using the decibel as a measure of comparison between power values.

Section 8.3 discusses equipment and proper methods for making basic electrical measurements, again taking advantage of the water flow model for ease of understanding. We will also learn a simple method of shifting electrical numerical values back-and-forth between all those confusing math prefixes, like milli-, micro-, mega-, and others. You'll be able to keep all those prefixes straight after Section 8.3 and shove pesky decimals around with great confidence!

8.1   It's Electric!
Electric Basics

Electricity in a Circuit is much like water flowing in plumbing. Instead of water molecules flowing in a pipe, electricity is electrons flowing in a conductor such as a wire. The basic measures of electricity can be likened to characteristics of water.

(TSA05) **Voltage (E) is the electrical term for the electromotive force (EMF) that causes electrons to flow.** *Voltage is like water pressure* in plumbing. High pressure pushes water current strongly through pipes; high voltage pushes electrons strongly through electrical conductors like copper wire.

(TSA06 TSA11) **Volt (v): The basic unit of electromotive force,** a measure of the "electron pressure." For instance, **a mobile transceiver usually requires about 12 volts to operate.**

Battery: A battery may be thought of as the water pump causing the electron pressure and inducing a flow of current, and higher voltage batteries provide higher pressure (voltage) just like a stronger water pump.

(TSA03) **Current (I) is the name for the flow of electrons in an electric circuit,** just as water current is the flow of water particles through a pipe or down a river.

(TSA01) **Ampere (A):** The basic unit of electrical current is the Ampere, or Amp (A). **Electrical current is measured in units of Amperes.**

(TSA04) **Direct Current (DC): Current that flows in only one direction** in a circuit. Direct current is typical of current flowing from a battery in which the electrons consistently move in one direction through a closed circuit.

(TSA12 TSA09) **Alternating Current (AC): Current that reverses direction on a regular basis in a circuit. The number of times per second that AC reverses direction is its frequency,** in units of hertz. Alternating current is typical of that from a household wall outlet. In the US, standard AC frequency is 60 hertz. In RF oscillators, alternating current for the production of radio signals will reverse direction many millions of times

each second to produce megahertz range frequencies of HF, VHF, UHF, and higher.

Conductors / Insulators: A good electrical conductor, such as copper, allows electrons to flow readily through it. **A good electrical insulator, such as glass,** allows no flow of electrons through it. Most electronic circuits use a combination of conductors, insulators, and *semi-conductors* (partially conducting materials whose conductivity may be changed in a controlled way).

Resistance (R) is the opposition to the flow of direct current (DC) in a circuit. You may think of resistance as a constriction or partial blockage in a water pipe and also as a device that forces the water to do work with the current, such as a water wheel driving a mill.

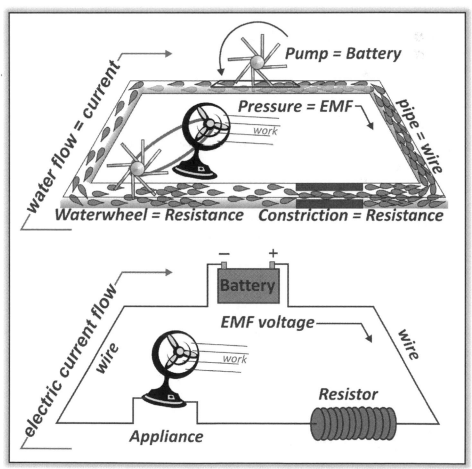

Figure 8.1: Water Flow Model of an Electrical Circuit

Ohm (Ω): The basic unit of resistance. (Also the basic unit of impedance.)

Appliances: All electrical appliances, such as light bulbs, heating elements, motors, or RF transmitters offer electrical resistance in the course of performing some work, just as the waterwheel offers resistance to water flow while doing its mechanical work.

Resistor: An electronic component that opposes the flow of electrical current through it, reducing the current flow (given a constant voltage) and transforming electrical energy from the resisted current into waste heat. A resistor is like a narrowing of the water pipe, or an obstacle in the pipe, constricting the allowable flow of current.

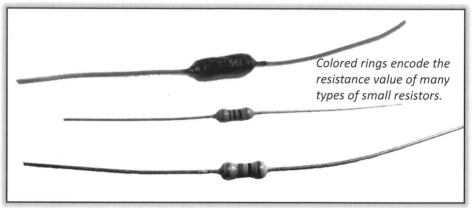

Colored rings encode the resistance value of many types of small resistors.

Figure 8.2: Example Resistors

Impedance: A measure of the opposition to the flow of alternating current (AC) in a circuit, expressed in **units of ohms.** Like resistance, impedance may be thought of as a blockage or constriction in the water pipe, or a device on which work is done by the alternating current. Since many RF circuits, such as the circuit comprised of your transmitter, feedline, and antenna, utilize alternating current at HF, VHF, and UHF frequencies, impedance has a significant impact on the operation of these circuits. (See Section 7.2, *SWR.*)

Are you getting a jolt from this organized lightning? Electricity is really more like water in pipes than wild flying lightning when it has been tamed to run through engineered circuits. More fun with electron flow is coming next, but try the *Section 8.1* questions first. You may be *shocked* by how much you've already learned!

www.HamRadioSchool.com/tech_media

It's Electric!

8.2   Ohm's Law and Power Law

> **❝** *Ohm found that the results could be summed up in such a simple law that he who runs may read it, and a schoolboy now can predict what Faraday then could only guess at roughly. – Oliver Heaviside*

Gee, you can read it even while running by. Must be pretty simple! And it really is. Two fundamental laws of electricity are key to understanding many aspects of your radio, from the way electronic circuits work to determining the capacity needed from your power supply or batteries. Ohm's Law defines a simple relationship among EMF (voltage), current, and resistance. The Power Law defines a relationship among electrical power, current, and EMF (voltage). If you can multiply and divide you are overqualified to apply these two laws.

Ohm's Law: E = I x R   Used to calculate voltage in a circuit.

T5D02

E is electromotive force (EMF), in volts.
I is current, in amps.
R is resistance, in Ohms.

With some very simple algebra you obtain the alternate forms of this relationship:

I = E ÷ R   and   **R = E ÷ I**

| T5D05 | T5D06 | T5D07 | T5D08 |
| T5D09 | T5D10 | T5D11 | T5D12 |

T5D01 T5D03

So, if you know any two of these quantities you can easily calculate the third. There are several questions in the Technician question pool about this relationship. Here is an easy visual tool to help you keep Ohm's Law straight and guarantee you answer the questions correctly:

Draw a capital 'T' inside a triangle to make three divisions and place the letters E, I, and R inside, like this. When an exam question asks for the value of one of these quantities, either

EMF, current, or resistance, it will always provide the other two quantities you need.

To use the Ohm's Law Triangle, cover the quantity being asked for and examine the two remaining ones. If the two remaining quantities are side-by-side, multiply them together for the answer. If the two quantities are one-above-the-other, divide the top one by the bottom one to get the answer. Here are a couple of examples right from the question pool.

T5D04

Q. What is the resistance of a circuit in which a current of 3 amperes flows through a resistor connected to 90 volts?

> **A. 3 ohms**   **C. 93 ohms**
> **B. 30 ohms**   **D. 270 ohms**

R (resistance) is asked for, so cover R in the triangle. Note that E (volts) and I (current in amperes) remain and are one-over-the-other, E / I. Divide:

    90 v ÷ 3 amps = **30 ohms**

The correct answer is 'B'.

T5D12

Q. What is the voltage across a 10-ohm resistor if a current of 2 amperes flows through it?

> **A. 8 volts**   **C. 12 volts**
> **B. 0.2 volts**   **D. 20 volts**

Voltage (v) is asked for, so cover the E. Note that I (current in amps) and R (resistance in ohms) remains, and they are side-by-side. Multiply:

    2 amps x 10 ohms = **20 volts**

The correct answer is 'D'.

The same method applies for all Ohm's Law questions. If current is asked for, cover the I and divide: E ÷ R ... That's 'volts ÷ ohms' to get current in amperes. Don't let variations in question wording trick you! Practice.

Ohm's Law Water Analogy: Think about Ohm's Law with the water analogy that we introduced in the last section. Remember that EMF (voltage) is like the water pressure pushing water through the plumbing pipes, while current (amperes) is like the quantity of water that flows through the pipes, perhaps in gallons per minute. Resistance (ohms) is like the diameter of the pipe, or the reduced room to flow if obstacles are in the pipe.

One expression of Ohm's Law is: I = E ÷ R. So the amount of water flowing (water current) is equal to the water pressure divided by the pipe resistance.

> If the water pressure is high, the amount of flow is high.
> If the water pressure is low, the amount of flow is low.
> If the pipe is wide open with tiny resistance, current is high.
> If the pipe is narrow and clogged, current is low.

This makes sense to anyone who has ever tried to take a shower while the dishwasher is running, the clothes washer is filling, and the kids are outside with the hose washing the dog. The water pressure is very low, so your shower is a dribble. But when the dishes and the dog are clean and the clothes washer completes its cycle, you get a blast of water with the increased pressure… Unless, of course, the corrosion in the pipes has plugged up the shower head offering high resistance. In that case you still get only a little water out. Bad day for a shower.

The Power Law is just as easy to use as Ohm's Law, and there is a handy visual tool for it, and a water analogy, too! Let's go there.

Power: the rate at which electrical energy is used. Electrical power is measured in units of watts.

Power Law: P = I x E   Used to calculate power in a DC circuit.

> P is power, in watts.
> I is current, in amps.
> E is electromotive force (EMF), in volts.

Just as with Ohm's Law, you can rearrange the relationship to be:

> E = P ÷ I   and   I = P ÷ E

Again like Ohm's Law, if you know any two of these quantities you can easily calculate the third. There are a few questions in the Technician question pool about this relationship also, and you can use the same kind of visual tool to remember the relationships:

T5A10 T5A02 T5C08

T5C10

Draw the same triangle form with divisions, but place the letters P, I, and E inside this time, with P up top. When an exam question asks for the value of one of these quantities, either power, current, or EMF, it will always provide the other two quantities you need.

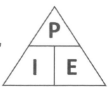

The same technique applies for using the Power Triangle: Cover the quantity being asked for, then multiply or divide the remaining two quantities depending on their position. If they're side-by-side, multiply. If one is over the other, divide the top by the bottom value. A couple of examples from the question pool never hurt…

Q. How much power is being used in a circuit when the applied voltage is 13.8 volts DC and the current is 10 amperes?

> **A. 138 watts**   **C. 23.8 watts**
> **B. 0.7 watts**   **D. 3.8 watts**

Power is asked for, so cover P, leaving I x E:
10 amps x 13.8v = **138 watts**

The correct answer is 'A.'

Q. How many amperes are flowing in a circuit when the applied voltage is 12 volts DC and the load is 120 watts?

> **A. 0.1 amperes**   **C. 12 amperes**
> **B. 10 amperes**   **D. 132 amperes**

Amperes is asked for, the unit of current (I).
Cover the I and divide P / E.
120 watts ÷ 12v = **10 amperes**

The correct answer is 'B.'

Power Water Analogy: The Power Law can be easily comprehended with a water analogy also. Power is a measure of how much work can be done over time by the electricity, or the water. The P = I x E relationship says that power is the result of multiplying the amount of water (current, I) by the water pressure (voltage, E).

A large volume of water (high current) can do a lot of work even if it is under low pressure (low voltage). Imagine an ocean wave slowly washing past you, shoving you back to shore, perhaps landing you on your bottom. The ocean current is not under high pressure, but it can sure do a lot of work pushing you around because the current is huge! Similarly, a lot of electrical current, such as that from a heavy duty automobile starting battery, can do a lot of work under the relatively low EMF of 12 volts.

On the other hand, imagine a fire hose blasting into your chest with a quick burst, putting you down on the ground a few feet backward, just like that ocean wave. Ouch! That's not a lot of water compared to the big wave, but it is under a lot of pressure, so it can do the same work as the wave. High voltage with relatively few electrons of current moving can have a big effect. Shuffle your rubber slippers across the carpet during a dry winter day then reach out for a grounded light switch or metal doorknob. ZAP! That static discharge may result from an EMF of several thousand volts, but the electrical current is tiny. It still will get your attention!

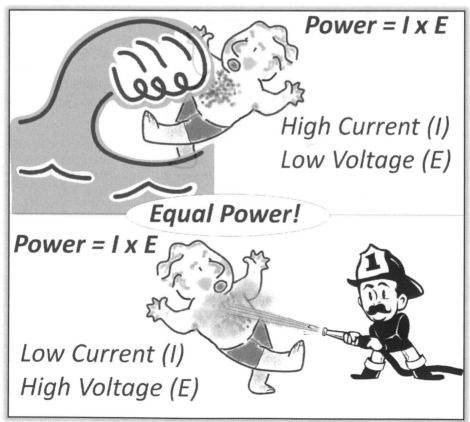

Figure 8.3: A Water Analogy for Power Law

Power Changes in decibels: A common calculation in RF applications involves determining power change, such as the change in the power of a signal received from another station. An indication of this is provided on a radio's signal strength meter, or "S-meter." As a rule of thumb, one unit of change on an S-meter is approximately 6 *decibels* of power change.

Uh… so what's a decibel?

Decibel (dB): A fractional logarithmic unit indicating a ratio of power or intensity relative to a reference level. A logarithmic scale for power is convenient because power values vary over a very wide range, and a logarithmic scale allows for easy comparisons, or ratios, across such a broad range.

A logarithmic scale means that each equally spaced unit on the scale changes in absolute measure by a factor of 10, such as the lower scale of Figure 8.4. The bel is a seldom used logarithmic ratio unit equating to a 10:1 ratio. Each increasing unit on the logarithmic scale equates to an increase of 1 bel.

"Deci" means 1/10, or 0.1. The decibel is 1/10 of a bel. So 10 decibels represents one bel, or one logarithmic unit of change, or a comparison ratio of 10:1 between two power values. This can be a little confusing if it has been a while since high school math, so here are two simple of rules of thumb that you can use to interpret power changes in decibels:

1. A doubling or halving of power (watts) is equal to a change of approximately 3 decibels. [3 dB = 2x, or 2:1 ratio]
2. A 10x change of power (watts) is equal to a change of 10 decibels. [10 dB = 10x, or a 10:1 ratio]

A couple of exam pool questions will help drive home how to use these rules of thumb.

Q. What is the approximate amount of change, measured in decibels (dB), of a power increase from 5 watts to 10 watts?

A. 2 dB	**C. 5 dB**
B. 3 dB	**D. 10 dB**

Check decibel rule #1: Power going from 5 watts to 10 watts is a doubling of power. A doubling of power is an increase of **3 dB**. The correct answer is 'B'. Remember, it is the comparison, or the ratio of the two values that counts in determining decibels, and not any absolute numerical value!

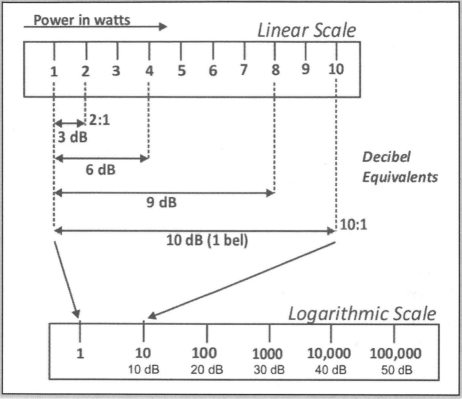

Figure 8.4: Relationship of Linear Scale to Logarithmic Scale

Q. What is the approximate amount of change, measured in decibels (dB), of a power decrease from 12 watts to 3 watts?

T5B10

A. -1 dB   C. -6 dB
B. -3 dB   D. -9 dB

This one is a little trickier. Again, apply decibel rule #1 like this: A halving of 12 watts is 6 watts; that's one 3 dB reduction, or -3 dB. A halving of 6 watts is 3 watts; that's another -3 dB change. The total decibel reduction from 12 watts to 3 watts is two "halving" steps, or two changes of -3 dB each, or **-6 dB** total change. The correct answer is 'C'.

Q. What is the approximate amount of change, measured in decibels (dB), of a power increase from 20 watts to 200 watts?

T5B11

A. 10 dB   C. 18 dB
B. 12 dB   D. 28 dB

Check decibel rule #2: Power changing from 20 to 200 watts is a factor of 10 increase (20 watts x 10 = 200 watts). That is a **10 dB** increase. The correct answer is 'A.'

Like I said, if you can multiply and divide numbers you are overqualified to apply Ohm's Law and the Power Law as a ham radio operator. Figuring out decibel logarithmic power changes isn't much tougher. And remember, that S-meter on your shiny new HT display tends to present approximately 6 dB per unit, so tell me… By what factor has your received signal power increased if you see a one S-unit increase? How about a 2 S-unit increase?

I hope you figured it out: One S-unit is 6 dB, or 2 x 3dB, so that's two power doublings which is about 4x the power. If 'P' is the starting power level:

    2 x P = 2P, and then
    2 x 2P = 4P

One S-unit is about a 4-fold change in power.

Two S-units is 12 dB, or 4 x 3dB, so four power doublings, like this:

    2 x P = 2P
    2 x 2P = 4P
    2 x 4P = 8P
    2 x 8P = 16P

That means approximately a 16-fold increase in signal strength!

Go *run* by the **Section 8.2** question pool for this section. *Ohm my!* You're developing some *powerful* number skills now!

www.HamRadioSchool.com/tech_media

8.3   It's Electric!

Making Electrical Measurements

> " *Benjamin Franklin may have discovered electricity, but it was the man who invented the meter who made the money.* – Earl Wilson

If you are ever going to apply any of the electrical knowledge you have accumulated so far, you should be able to properly measure electricity. It's a good skill to have that will come in handy in many situations. We can use the water analogy of electricity to reason out how to make some electrical measurements, and we can use the goofy little rhyme learned back in the Section 4.1, *Wavelength and Frequency*, to switch between different magnitudes and prefixes used with electrical measures.

First, let's take a look at the various types of instruments used to measure the basic electrical characteristics we have learned about.

Instruments: Each of the electrical quantities in Ohm's Law – EMF (in volts), current (in amperes), and resistance (in ohms) – can be measured with a unique electrical instrument.

Voltmeter: An instrument used to measure electrical potential or electromotive force is a voltmeter. Using the water analogy, we can see that **the correct way to connect a voltmeter to a circuit is in parallel with the circuit.** Think of the voltmeter allowing just a little of the water from a high pressure location to squirt through the measuring device and flow out to a lower pressure position in the circuit, as in Figure 8.5 on the next page. If there is a water pressure difference between the 'inflow' location and the 'outflow' location, the water will surge through the measuring device and cause it to register the pressure difference, or in this case, the electrical potential difference or EMF. **Take precaution when measuring high voltages that the voltmeter and leads are rated for use at the voltages to be measured,** or the voltmeter may be damaged and the leads may overheat!

Ammeter: An instrument used to measure electrical current is an ammeter. Again, the water analogy shows the correct connection technique:

T7D01 T7D02

T7D12

T7D04

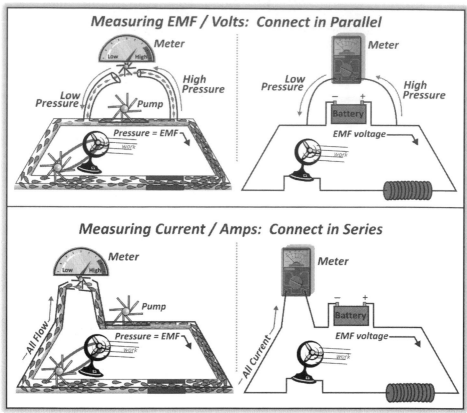

Figure 8.5: Measuring EMF / Volts vs. Current / Amps

T7D03 **An ammeter is usually connected to a circuit in series with the circuit.** Since you are measuring current, or the amount of water that is flowing, you have to let all the water flow through the measuring device or you will miss some of it! So, connect in series such that all the flowing electrons are routed through the ammeter.

T7D05 Ohmmeter: **An instrument used to measure resistance is an ohmmeter.** An ohmmeter is usually connected across the resistive element, whether a simple resistor or an appliance being driven within the circuit. You may think of the ohmmeter as squirting a little water of a specific pressure (voltage) through the resistive element and measuring how much current gets through it. Then, using Ohm's Law where R = E ÷ I, resistance in ohms is calculated from the known voltage (E) and the measured current (I). (Note: An ohmmeter may also use the reverse technique of a known input current and measured voltage drop to compute resistance.)

T7D11 **Ohmmeter Precautions:** You may have already realized from that last paragraph that **when measuring circuit resistance with an ohmmeter you**

should take precaution to ensure that the circuit is not powered.
This makes sense because the ohmmeter relies upon its own known input voltage for accurate resistance measurement. If there is another voltage applied to the circuit the measurement will be erroneous.

The situation above can also happen if electric charge is stored in the circuit within a component called a *capacitor*. We will learn more about capacitors in the next section, but think of it like a small battery that can temporarily store electrical energy, and when the circuit is completed it discharges the current into the circuit. **If an ohmmeter is connected across a circuit and initially indicates a low resistance and then shows increasing resistance with time, what is probably happening is that the circuit contains a large capacitor** that is discharging through the ohmmeter. The extra current and voltage of the capacitor fools the ohmmeter into thinking its own provided current is flowing quite freely with very low resistance, and as the capacitor's charge is exhausted the ohmmeter corrects to the higher resistance reading that results from only its own stable current through the resistor.

Multimeter: A common instrument available at any hardware store is the *multimeter*. As the name implies, it provides the capability of measuring multiple electrical characteristics. **A multimeter is commonly used to make measurements of voltage and resistance,** as well as current (amperage).

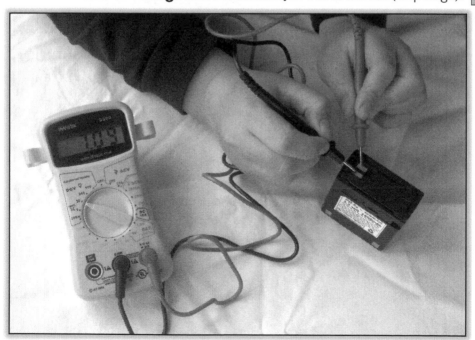

Figure 8.6: Measuring Radio Battery Voltage with a Multimeter

A multimeter allows the user to select the type of measurement to be made, usually with a simple dial or push-button control. But some caution is warranted when using a multimeter to make sure you have selected the correct measurement setting for the type of measurement you intend to make. **A multimeter might be damaged by attempting to measure voltage when using the resistance setting.** This scenario might allow high current to flow through sensitive circuits in the multimeter that are designed to measure only the small, instrument-provided currents for resistance measuring, just as with an ohmmeter. Putting higher voltage pressure behind those circuits and pushing a lot of current through them may result in an electronic component burning out!

Units and Prefixes: Just as with the broad range of radio frequencies, the breadth of electrical measurement magnitudes require that we use prefixes for convenience to denote thousands, millions, or billions of units, or on the smaller side of one, thousandths, millionths, billionths, or even trillionths of units. As noted at the start of this section, that extremely cheesy little rhyme can help us here, too:

> *From hefty to slight, dot moves right. From slight to hefty, dot's a lefty.*

> *Now learn prefixes from hefty to slight, left to right,*
> *And slather rhyming cheeses on the Tech pool teases!*
> *Sling that techno-speak like a savvy geek,*
> *And measure electricity with simplicity!*

Uh, geez, sorry, that just slipped out. It won't happen again. I promise. I have no future as a hip-hop rap star, huh?

Less than One: Where values get smaller than one, the prefixes and their meanings are as follows, slight (smaller) to hefty (larger):

pico	one trillionth	1/1,000,000,000,000	0.000000000001
nano	one billionth	1/1,000,000,000	0.000000001
micro	**one millionth**	1/1,000,000	0.000001
milli	one thousandth	1/1,000	0.001
	unity		1

More than One: Where values get big, you will recognize these prefixes and their meanings from previous sections. Continuing in slight to hefty sequence, picking up at unity value (1):

	unity	1
kilo	**one thousand**	1,000
mega	one million	1,000,000
giga	one billion	1,000,000,000

T5B03

That's about as far as we need to go, as these are the most common prefixes you will encounter in amateur radio. Be aware, there are more, greater and smaller.

You may want to create your own mnemonic phrase to remember this sequence, slight to hefty, as presented above. Or, you can use my *assassin shopping* mnemonic, with apology for the violent imagery an inelegance:

Pick from **Nan, Mic,** or **Milli, One** to **Kill Meg** & **Gigi.**

I'm sure you will pick right up on the sequence represented as pico-nano-micro-milli-one-kilo-mega-giga. This includes unity, or 1, to help keep straight that important positional relationship. However, I really don't advocate violence against anyone named Meg or Gigi.

Now, from Pick-to-Gigi, let's slather some of that rhyming cheese and solve a few examples directly from the Technician question pool.

Q. How many milliamperes is 1.5 amperes?
    A. 15 milliamperes   **C. 1,500 milliamperes**
    B. 150 milliamperes   **D. 15,000 milliamperes**

T5B01

Always place the known quantity on the left before slathering cheese, just to keep your brain straight. Like this: *1.5 amperes = ? milliamperes*

Ampere is the unity value 1, and milliamperes is smaller (slighter) than 1. Just like before, we move the decimal point in the proper direction 3 places for each prefix step. There is only one step between unity (1) ampere and milliampere (one thousandth). That's from 'One' to 'Milli.'

You may now apply the cheese:
    From hefty to slight, dot moves right! Right 3 places, like this:
        1.5 amperes = 1,500 milliamperes
    The correct answer is 'C.'

Q. How many microfarads are 1,000,000 picofarads?
A. 0.001 microfarads   **C. 1000 microfarads**
B. 1 microfarad   **D. 1,000,000,000 microfarads**

Again, the known quantity to the left, then determine the number of prefix steps and size relationship, and last the glorious cheese:

> 1,000,000 picofarads = ? microfarads
> Pico to micro is 2 prefix steps, or 6 places, from smaller to larger.
> From slight to hefty, dot's a lefty! (Move decimal left 6 places.)
> **1,000,000 picofarads = 1 microfarad**   Answer 'B' is correct.

One more, just for fun:

Q. If an ammeter calibrated in amperes is used to measure a 3000-milliampere current, what reading would it show?
A. 0.003 amperes   **C. 3 amperes**
B. 0.3 amperes   **D. 3,000,000 amperes**

Don't let the framing of the question trick you. It is a basic conversion. Follow the same procedure, starting with the known quantity:

> 3,000 milliamperes = ? amperes
> Milli to unity (1) is one prefix step, smaller to larger.
> From slight to hefty, dot's a lefty!
> **3,000 milliamperes = 3 amperes.**   'C' is correct.

Almost done… Just one last thing… Kind of a leftover electrical topic…

Battery Types: Before we depart from our electrical discussion, we must address a few points about batteries. Virtually every HT radio uses batteries, and most ham radios can be operated on battery power. This is one of the advantages of ham radio for emergency preparedness, after all. We don't need no stinkin' power grid!

Carbon-Zinc: *Carbon-zinc* and the closely related *alkaline* batteries are what you probably think of as just plain old generic batteries – nothing special, and they drain pretty quickly. Carbon-zinc is an older battery technology now infrequently utilized in amateur radio. **Carbon-zinc batteries are not rechargeable,** nor are their alkaline cousins.

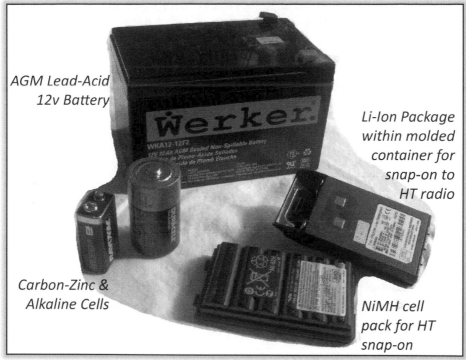

AGM Lead-Acid
12v Battery

Li-Ion Package
within molded
container for
snap-on to
HT radio

Carbon-Zinc &
Alkaline Cells

NiMH cell
pack for HT
snap-on

Figure 8.7: Various Battery Types Used in Amateur Radio

Nickel-Metal Hydride (NiMH): These batteries and the older, similar nickel-cadmium (NiCad) cells **are rechargeable batteries** still in common use with many amateur radios. Most NiMH batteries are sealed packages containing multiple individual cells. They are well suited for amateur radio use because they can provide high surge currents for transmitting power.

Lithium-Ion: *Lithium-ion* cells are becoming very popular due to their high charge densities, or ability to store larger amounts of energy than other battery types. This allows them to be smaller and lighter than other cell types for the same capacity or time of use. Many modern HT radios employ *Li-ion* batteries. **Lithium-Ion batteries are rechargeable.**

Lead-Acid: Although very old technology, **lead-acid is a rechargeable battery type** still commonly used. Variations known as '*gel cells*' or *AGM* (absorbed glass mat) are frequently used in amateur radio for portable operations, for emergency backup power, or as a primary power source. Lead-acid cells provide excellent surge currents for transmitting power. They are also very cost effective, but lead-acid batteries have a relatively low energy-to-weight ratio; they're heavy, but they are reliable. **One way to recharge a 12-volt lead-acid station battery if commercial power is out is to**

T6A10

T2C02

connect the battery in parallel with a vehicle's battery and run the engine.

The *Absorbed Glass Mat* (AGM) battery holds the electrolyte in glass matting rather than a flowing liquid like common lead-acid cells. This helps make the cells safer if damaged, less prone to leakage or spilling, and essentially maintenance free except for charging. AGM batteries are more expensive than liquid electrolytic lead-acid cells, and they require "smart charger" technology to avoid overcharging that will cause the AGM cell to fail prematurely. The smart charger senses the battery charge level and adjusts the charging current to an optimized profile over the charge time, ending with a maintenance "trickle charge" to keep the battery at maximum charge state without damaging it.

Time now to measure your electrical success. Work through the questions for **Section 8.3** and then come back for some electronic wonderment in the next section. If you have never understood what those little components in your electronic devices actually do and how they work, we are going to begin to absolve you of that innocence next!

www.HamRadioSchool.com/tech_media

Bonus Question from the Tech Pool:

TSB05

Q. Which of the following is equivalent to 500 milliwatts?
A. 0.02 watts   **C. 5 watts**
B. 0.5 watts   **D. 50 watts**

500 milliwatts = ? watts
Dot moves 3 places left. (Going slight to hefty one step.)
Correct answer is **0.5 watts** (B).

9.0	Hamtronics

❝ *When I was a teenager in the late 30's and early 40's, electronics wasn't a word. You were interested in radio if you were interested in electronics. – Ken Olson*

Electronics remain at the heart of radio today. Many radio amateurs enjoy wielding a hot soldering iron to piece together electronic components on a printed circuit board. One of the FCC's stated purposes in Part 97 for establishing the Amateur Radio Service is to expand the reservoir of trained electronics experts [Part 97.1(d)]. Although it isn't absolutely necessary for daily radio operations to comprehend the incredible manipulation of electrons taking place in the palm of your hand, it is good to be familiar with the basics of electronics for troubleshooting, for safety, and simply for expanding your understanding of radio.

And then there is the Technician question pool in which about 12% of the 420+ questions relate to electronics and electronic concepts. You will typically encounter about four electronics questions on your exam, so let's get at this topic with gusto! With the knowledge you have accumulated in the last few sections it will be a piece of cake.

In Section 9.1 we will discuss basic electronics concepts and learn the names, symbols, and elementary functions of some of the most common electronic components such as *resistors*, *capacitors*, and *diodes*. We will examine the effect that each of these components has on the flow of electrons in a circuit.

In Section 9.2 we will expand the discussion to a special electronic component called the *transistor*, and we will consider a couple of basic electronic circuits constructed from the various components learned in Section 9.1. We will also cover a couple of basics about soldering these components together to form circuits.

Hamtronics

9.1 Electronic Basics

The Big Picture: Radio electronics are comprised of individual electronic components linked together to form complex circuits in which electron flow is manipulated. Each component is precision manufactured with specialized materials, most commonly *semiconductors*, and each component serves a unique function in the manipulation of voltage, current, resistance, impedance, and other electrical waveform characteristics.

T6D09 **A device that combines several semiconductors and other components into one package is called an integrated circuit** (IC). An integrated circuit may perform a wide variety of tasks, including transmitting and receiving radio signals.

Semiconductor: One of several types of material with electrical conductivity in between that of a conductor and that of an insulator. These materials are used to create a variety of electronic components such as transistors, diodes, resistors, and others. Sometimes the term 'semiconductor' is used to refer generally to the class of electronic components made from these materials, as in the highlighted text above.

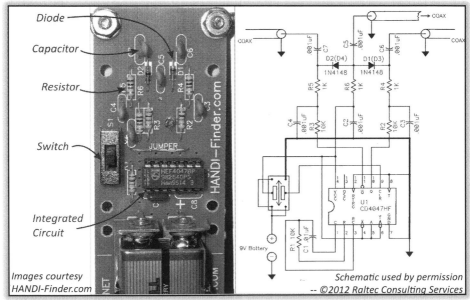

Figure 9.1: Printed Circuit Board with IC and Schematic Diagram

Schematic Symbols: The standardized representations of components in an electrical wiring diagram are schematic symbols. Each symbol on an electrical circuit schematic diagram represents an electrical component. An electrical circuit schematic diagram accurately represents only the way components are interconnected. The connecting wire lengths shown in a schematic diagram are not usually accurate, and the symbols do not depict a true physical appearance of the electronic components.

Electronic Components manipulate the flow of electrons, or current, in a circuit as well as the EMF or voltage across portions of the circuit. Some electrical components are combined in specific ways to change AC current to DC current, to produce radio frequency AC current oscillations, to alter the amplitude, frequency, or phase of an RF signal, and to perform other functions that make radio communications possible. Some electrical components simply emit light and serve as a visual indicator on your radio, such as a "Power On" light. Electronic components include *resistors, capacitors, inductors, diodes* and more! Let's take a closer look at some of these.

Resistor: An electrical component used to oppose the flow of current in a DC circuit is a resistor. Given a constant voltage, resistors reduce current flow in accordance with Ohm's Law (Section 8.2).

> **Potentiometer or Variable Resistor:** An electronic component in which the amount of resistance it provides in a circuit may be varied across a specified range of values. The change in the value of a potentiometer is often accomplished by physically manipulating a control. **A potentiometer is often used as an adjustable volume control** on a radio, for instance. **A potentiometer controls resistance.**

> **Symbols:** The symbol for a simple resistor is a zig-zag line. An arrow added to the zig-zag line and pointing into it is the symbol for a variable resistor.

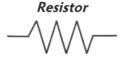
Resistor

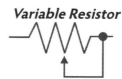
Variable Resistor

Capacitor: An electrical component that stores energy in an electric field is a capacitor. A capacitor consists of two or more conductive surfaces separated by an insulator. The ability to store energy in an electric field is called capacitance, and the basic unit of capacitance is the farad.

Symbols: The symbol for a capacitor is two lines separated a short distance and oriented perpendicular to the circuit wiring connections. Usually, but not always, one of the lines is curved slightly. A variable capacitor with which capacitance may be adjusted to different values will typically have an arrow depicted angled over the capacitor symbol.

T6C06

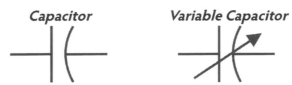

Capacitor   *Variable Capacitor*

Structure and Behavior: A capacitor may consist of metal foils separated by a layer of insulating film. When a voltage is applied across the conducting surfaces a static electric field builds up across the insulating layer and causes a positive charge to collect on one conductor and a negative charge on the other conductor. A capacitor tends to oppose DC currents because it is effectively a gap or opening in the circuit, and DC current will cross the insulated gap only if the charge builds up and the electric potential across the gap is great enough to cause a 'jump' of charge. Capacitors tend to offer reduced opposition to AC currents since the static electric charges it creates on each conductor can build and drain repeatedly as the current reverses direction each cycle.

T6A06 T6A07 T5C03 T5C04

Inductor: An electrical component that stores energy in a magnetic field is an inductor. An inductor is usually composed of a coil of wire. The ability to store energy in a magnetic field is called inductance, and the basic unit of inductance is the henry.

Symbols: The symbol for an inductor is a 'humped' line reminiscent of a coil. A variable inductor with which inductance may be adjusted to different values will add an arrow pointing into the inductor symbol.

T6C10

Inductor   *Variable Inductor*

Structure and Behavior: An inductor is composed of a coil of wire, frequently coiled around a metal core or a toroid that provides enhanced performance. As current flows through the coil a magnetic field is induced around the coil, and the expansion or contraction of the magnetic field imposes some opposition to current flow since the expansion and contraction of the field does work. Inductors tend to oppose AC currents because the reversal of current direction causes repeated expansion and contraction of the magnetic field with alternating directions of magnetic field lines (magnetic field directionality depends upon current direction). Inductors tend to offer little or no opposition to DC currents following the initial current flow's build-up of the magnetic field since with DC current the magnetic field is stable.

Diode: An electronic component that allows current to flow in only one direction is a diode.

Symbol: The symbol for a diode is a triangle with a straight line across the triangle point that lies on the wiring line.

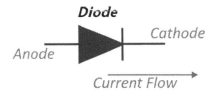

Diode

Cathode

Anode

Current Flow

Structure and Behavior: A diode has two electrode leads called the anode and the cathode. Current is allowed to flow in the direction of anode-to-cathode, but not in the opposite direction. **The semiconductor diode's cathode lead is usually identified with a stripe** around the component's circumference that is mirrored in a schematic diagram by the line on the diode's symbol.

Light Emitting Diode (LED): A special diode that emits light when 'forward biased' or when current flows in its allowable direction. **LEDs are commonly used as visual indicators** on displays or electronics.

Symbol: The symbol for a light emitting diode (LED) is a diode symbol with small arrows added that point away from the triangle at an angle, reminiscent of rays of light emitted from the diode. The small arrows may be straight or "zig-zag" style.

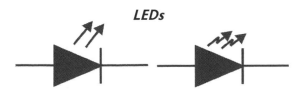

LEDs

more electronic components and more schematic symbols to learn, a little about how some components can work together to perform jobs. Check out the summary chart below and then take a break and make sure you have absorbed everything so far by hitting the question bank for **Section 9.1**. We'll pick up with the topic of transistors and additional component symbols in the next section.

www.HamRadioSchool.com/tech_media

Summary of Electronic Components from Section 9.1

Component	Parameter	Functions	Example
Resistor	Resistance (R) unit ohm	Opposes the flow of current in a DC circuit	
Potentiometer or Variable Resistor	Resistance (R) unit ohm	Commonly used as an adjustable volume control	
Capacitor	Capacitance unit farad	Stores energy in an electric field	
Inductor	Inductance unit henry	Stores energy in a magnetic field	
Diode	No unit of measure; leads are anode and cathode	Allows current to flow in only one direction	
LED: Light Emitting Diode	No unit of measure; a special type of diode	LED is commonly used as a visual indicator	

" *We believe that electricity exists, because the electric company keeps sending us bills for it, but we cannot figure out how it travels inside wires. – Dave Barry*

Of course, we really have figured out how electricity travels inside wires and we have learned to control it pretty well. One of the most useful electronic components for controlling electricity traveling in wires is the *transistor*, and we will focus on it in the first part of this section. We will also briefly review some more commonly known electronic components and their schematic symbols, such as switches, fuses, and lamps. We will finish up our electronic exploration with some odds and ends about groups of components that make circuits and some facts about soldering.

Transistor: A class of electronic components capable of using a voltage or current signal to control current flow. A transistor can be used as an electronic switch or as a signal amplifier. Amplification occurs when a controlling signal is input into the transistor such that it allows a larger current flow to continue through the transistor. However, a controlling signal may also be input that allows no current at all to flow, thereby making the transistor an electronic switch to turn on or off another electric current routed through the transistor.

T6B01 T6B03 T6B05

Structure and Behavior: A transistor is usually made of three layers of semiconductor material. The specific types of semiconductor materials are N-type that promotes an excess of negative charge accumulation, and P-type that promotes an excess of positive charge accumulation. These materials are sandwiched in PNP or NPN layers to create a transistor, and when currents are applied to the individual layers their charge interactions produce the unique transistor behaviors.

T6B04

A transistor has three *electrode leads*, or *terminals*, for connecting each of the layers in a circuit. A voltage or a current applied to one of the terminals controls the current flowing via the other two terminals. In other words, the current flowing through the transistor varies in magnitude as dictated by the controlling signal. The power of the controlled current can be much greater than the power of the controlling current, so a transistor effectively amplifies a signal that is used as the controlling signal. **A transistor's ability to amplify a signal is called gain.** (The concept of gain applies to transistors as well as to antennas, although in this case there is no 'directionality' of signal propagation as that producing antenna gain.)

Water Analogy: Yep, our old friend the water analogy applies to the action of transistors too, as in Figure 9.2 below. You may think of a transistor as an in-line plumbing valve that controls a large, high pressure flow of water in a pipe. Your manipulations of the valve, very weak in comparison to the power available in the strong flow of water, are like the low power controlling signals sent into the transistor. You can change the volume and power of the water flowing over time by making changes to the valve position over time. Imagine that you quickly open and close the valve several times in sequence – your weak valve signals are amplified into similar pulses in the powerful flow of water current through the pipe. The amount of this signal amplification is the gain.

Two types of transistors are commonly used:
1) Bipolar Junction Transistor (BJT) and 2) Field Effect Transistor (FET).

Bipolar Junction Transistor (BJT): The BJT, whether **PNP or NPN transistor** arrangement, has three terminals (or **electrodes**) that are called:
1. **Base** – the electrode to which a controlling current is applied.
2. **Collector** – one of the electrodes through which larger current flow occurs
3. **Emitter** – one of the electrodes through which larger current flow occurs, and through which the base controlling current is also routed.

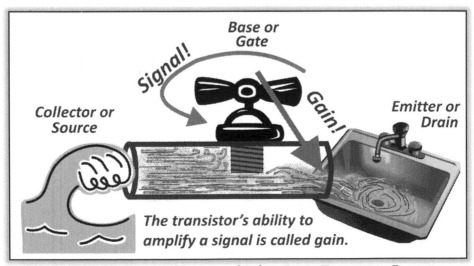

Figure 9.2: Water Analogy Applied to Basic Transistor Function

BJT Symbol: A transistor symbol is a circle with three lines extending from it to represent the three electrode connections, and a "pi-like" symbol within the circle. The BJT internal symbol typically depicts slanted legs of the pi-like symbol inside the circle.

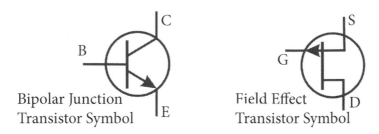

Bipolar Junction
Transistor Symbol

Field Effect
Transistor Symbol

Field Effect Transistor (FET): The FET uses an electric field to vary the size of a channel in its P-type and N-type semiconductor materials. Current flow is varied according to the channel's size or width. Different from the BJT, a controlling voltage signal is applied rather than a controlling current signal.

The FET has three electrodes that are called:
   1. Gate – the electrode to which a controlling voltage is applied.
   2. Source – one electrodes through which larger current flow occurs.
   3. Drain – one electrodes through which larger current flow occurs.

Symbols: FET symbols vary depending upon subtype, but are usually distinguished by the right-angle or squared nature of the pi-like symbol lines. Transistors are marvels of semiconductor electronics and used in virtually every electronic device imaginable. Their ability to amplify signals is particularly useful in radio where weak signals must be boosted through the various stages of transmission and reception, as described in Chapter 6, *How Radio Works*.

More Components and Symbols: Let's take a look at some additional electronic components that are probably a little more familiar to you, along with their schematic symbols.

Lamp: A simple filament based bulb that emits light when a current is passed through it.

Lamp

Battery: A chemical based source of electrical power.

Battery

Antenna: The RF radiating element of a radio system. The symbol resembles an inverted coat hanger.

Antenna

T6A08 **Switch: A component used to connect or disconnect an electrical circuit.** The simplest switch is termed "*single-pole, single-throw*" meaning that there is only one contact for the switch to make when closed (single pole) and only one lever to move (single throw). More complex switch designs may incorporate multiple contacts or multiple levers, as illustrated in the schematic symbols below.

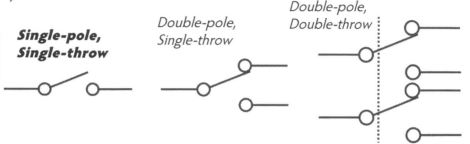

T6D03 **Single-pole, Single-throw**

Double-pole, Single-throw

Double-pole, Double-throw

T6D02 **Relay: A switch controlled by an electromagnet,** usually thrown by providing or removing current from the electromagnet's coil. As discussed in Section 9.1, a coil, or *inductor*, creates a magnetic field when current flows through it. This magnetic effect can be employed as an electromagnet to open or close a switch with magnetic force. This switch arrangement is called a *relay*.

T6A09 **Fuse: Used to protect other circuit components from current overloads.** If excessive current flows through the fuse, a narrow conductor or wire within the fuse will overheat and break, stopping the flow of current through the fuse.

Fuse

T6D04 **Meter: Used to display signal strength on a numeric scale.** Meters may include a needle pointer and scale or an electronic digit readout using LED or *liquid crystal display* (*LCD*) numerical characters.

T6D05 **Regulator: A type of circuit that controls the amount of voltage from a power supply.** A *regulated power supply* helps protect sensitive circuits in your radio from spikes and variations of voltage.

T6D06 **Transformer:** Used to convert from one voltage to another in a circuit. **Commonly used to change 120v AC house current to a lower AC voltage for other uses.** A transformer uses two coils (inductors) of different numbers of wire windings, each usually with metal core bars. Magnetic induction from one coil induces a current in the other with a voltage change proportional to the difference in winding numbers between the coils. The symbol for a transformer is a simplified

T6C09 representation of its physical form with inductors and core bars.

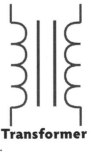

Transformer

Integrating Components Into Circuits: By combining the components listed in this section and the last, many useful circuits or circuit portions may be constructed. Here are three good examples for your consideration.

1. Rectifier: A device or circuit that changes an alternating current into a direct current signal. A rectifier uses multiple diodes to make the conversion from AC to DC current. Diodes are arranged in a circuit to provide two one-way paths for current such that both AC current directions result in current moving in only a single direction for output or application to a load (appliance). Compare the arrow paths of figure 9.3 depicting the two directions of AC current through the rectifier circuit.

T6D01

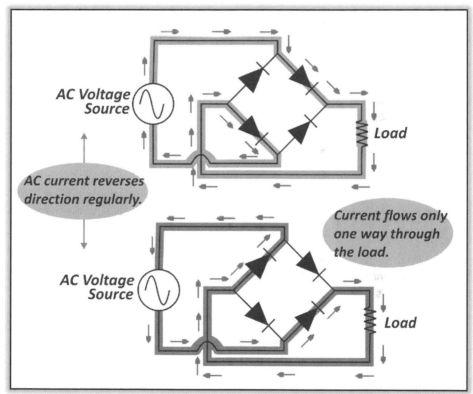

Figure 9.3: Two AC Current Paths of a Diode Rectifier Circuit

2. Tuned Circuit: Connected in series or parallel, an inductor and a capacitor can form a filter, or simple *tuned* or *resonant* circuit. A *tuned circuit* allows current to flow back and forth between the inductor and the capacitor, alternatively storing and releasing energy as a magnetic field (inductor) and an electric field (capacitor). The values of inductance and capacitance in the components of the tuned circuit may be selected so that the back-and-forth oscillations of AC current occur at a desired fre-

T6D08 T6D11

quency, such as a specific RF frequency. Tuned circuits may form the basis of RF oscillators in a radio, or they can be used to filter or select for only certain ranges of frequencies. The frequency of oscillation for a tuned circuit is called its *resonant frequency*, or *frequency of resonance*.

Here is a simplified diagram of a tuned circuit for receiving RF signals. The antenna sends signals received to the circuit. The tuned circuit has a vari-

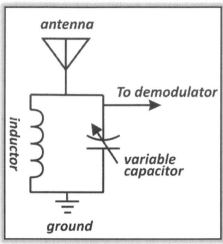

Figure 9.4: Simple Tuned Circuit

able capacitor whose value may be changed to select a resonant frequency for the circuit. With only a little RF signal from the antenna at the tuned frequency value, the circuit will begin to resonate, sending current alternatively clockwise and counterclockwise, building up the capacitor's electric field and then discharging to build up the inductor's magnetic field, repeatedly. This resonating signal can then be tapped by the demodulating circuit of the receiver for signal processing, as discussed in Section 6.2, *Receiving*.

3. Control Circuit: Many different arrangements of components are used to form circuits for the control of devices. One simple circuit uses a transistor to control the brightness of a lamp, as shown here from the Technician question pool diagrams.

The E-shaped symbols facing downward are electrical ground, so you may consider those positions all commonly connected. The V-shaped symbols on the far left indicate connections to other sources or circuits – in this case providing a controlling current through **resistor #1** to transistor #2's base electrode. **The BJT transistor, component #2, functions to control the flow**

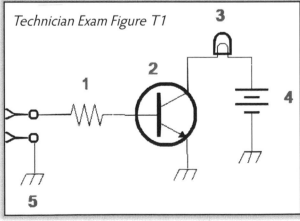

Figure 9.5: Control Circuit for a Lamp

of current from the **battery #4,** through the **lamp #3,** and ultimately through its collector and emitter electrodes out to electrical ground. As the controlling current is varied on the transistor the current allowed through the lamp varies commensurately, thereby controlling the lamp's brightness.

Printed Circuit Boards: Electronic circuits are commonly constructed on *printed circuit boards* (*PCBs*) where the electrode wires or leads of components are mounted in contact with a pattern of conducting material that has been printed onto the board. The thin printed pattern of conductive material serves the same function as wires connecting the components together in the manner prescribed by a schematic diagram. A common method of mounting components onto a PCB is by inserting the component terminal wires through small holes in the PCB and *soldering* the wires to the opposite side of the board in contact with the conductive pattern printed there.

Solder: *Solder* is a metal blend that melts at relatively low temperatures and provides excellent electrical conductivity. Common solder blends include the metals lead and tin, and frequently a small amount of silver. Solder is used to join conductors (wires, components leads, PCB pads) by heating the conductors briefly with a small iron, thereby causing the solder to melt, and then cool to solidify firmly around the conductors.

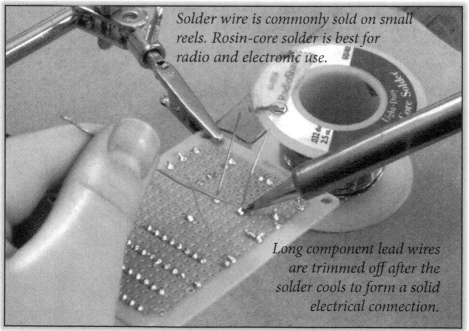

Solder wire is commonly sold on small reels. Rosin-core solder is best for radio and electronic use.

Long component lead wires are trimmed off after the solder cools to form a solid electrical connection.

Figure 9.6: Soldering Components "Through-the-Hole" on a PCB

T7D08 **Rosin-Core Solder is best for radio and electronic use.** A center core of *rosin* spreads around the solder joint and helps reduce oxidation that erodes the integrity of a soldered joint over time.

T7D09 **Cold Solder Joint: A grainy or dull surface on a solder joint is characteristic of a "cold" solder joint,** and it indicates that the solder joint did not form properly, warranting removal, cleaning, and resoldering of the joint to ensure a solid electrical connection. A good solder joint is usually smooth and shiny.

And that's how electricity flows through wires, under complete control by a bunch of electronic components just like the ones we've learned about in these last two section. If you have followed most of the discussion in these two sections, you now are more educated about electronics than 95% of your fellow citizens. Congratulations! Now go prove your 5% status with the rest of the Technician questions about electronics for **Section 9.2**. Good luck!

www.HamRadioSchool.com/tech_media

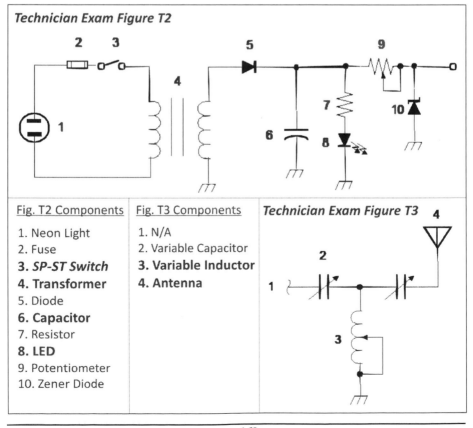

Technician Exam Figure T2

Fig. T2 Components	Fig. T3 Components
1. Neon Light	1. N/A
2. Fuse	2. Variable Capacitor
3. SP-ST Switch	**3. Variable Inductor**
4. Transformer	**4. Antenna**
5. Diode	
6. Capacitor	
7. Resistor	
8. LED	
9. Potentiometer	
10. Zener Diode	

Technician Exam Figure T3

10.0 Digital Modes

❝ *I do not fear computers. I fear
the lack of them. – Isaac Asimov*

Do not fear a computer in your ham shack! Ham radio and computers go together like ham and eggs. **A computer may be used as part of your amateur station for logging contacts and information, for generating and decoding digital signals, and even for sending and receiving CW!** Indeed, you should fear the lack of a computer connected to your rig, or at least realize you're missing out on some very cool ham action without one.

Digital Mode: A digital mode in amateur radio is one of several methods of communication in which information is encoded into digital form for transmission. Amateur radio **digital communication methods include packet, PSK31, MFSK,** automatic packet reporting (APRS), keyboard-to-keyboard text messaging, and even good ol' Morse Code. And more that you'll learn about in this section! Digital form may be thought of as a sequence or pattern of on/off signals or discrete signal changes representing binary characters (as in 1 / 0 sequences).

International Morse Code is used when sending CW in the amateur bands. This first-ever digital mode transmits a binary code via continuous wave (unmodulated) transmissions. **Any of the following may be used to transmit CW in the amateur bands:**

Straight Key: A vertical spring-lever arm that may be finger tapped or pressed to make an electrical contact for the transmission of CW signals.

Electronic Keyer: Devices of a variety of designs that electronically produce CW signals of consistent duration and tone for the "dit" (dot) and the "dah" (dash) of Morse Code. Keyers are often used with paddle or touch key input devices, facilitating separate operator input actions for dit or dah via a pair of paddles or touch sensitive contacts. The electronic keyer outputs a dit or dah with appropriate operator keying input.

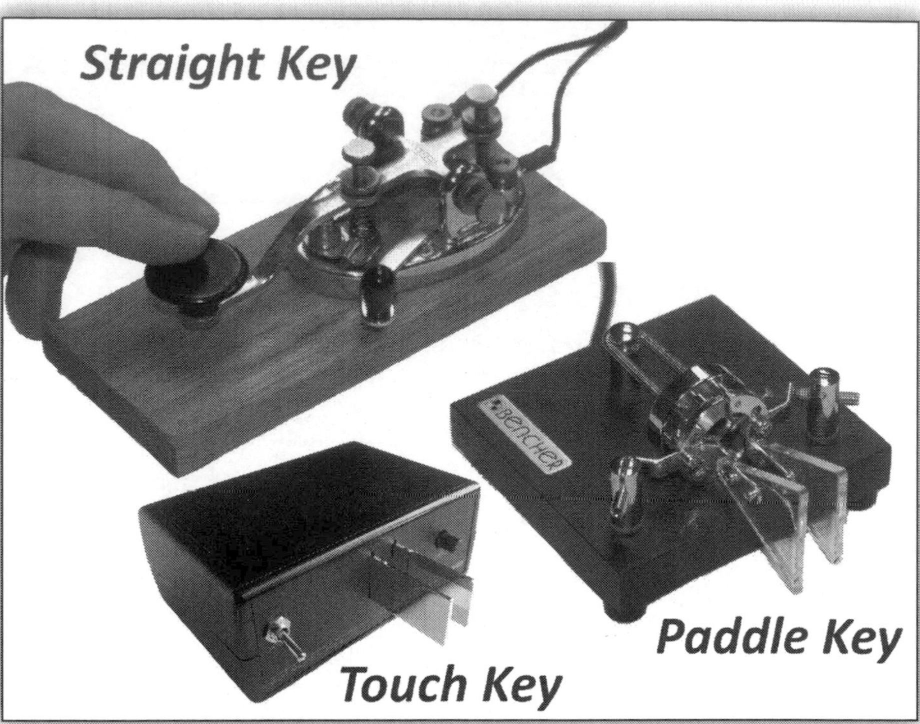

Straight Key

Paddle Key

Touch Key

Figure 10.1: Example Morse Code Keys for CW Transmitting

Computer Keyboard: With a proper computer interface, keyboard keystrokes may be converted into CW Morse Code signals for transmission. Similarly, software may be used to translate received Morse Code into on-screen computer text.

Packet: Packet Radio is a digital communication method used primarily with FM modulation on VHF and UHF bands to transmit digital data including email and text (keyboard to keyboard) messaging.

T4A06

Terminal Node Controller (TNC): A hardware 'box' **connected between a transceiver and computer in a packet radio station** to control the transmission and reception of digitally encoded messages. A TNC is much like a computer MODEM that connects one computer to another or to the internet via telephone lines, only the TNC connects via a radio transceiver. Some modern radios are sold with a TNC already integrated into the radio electronics.

T8D06 **T8D07**

PSK31: Phase Shift Keying 31 is a low-rate data transmission mode for keyboard-to-keyboard text messaging that works well in the noisy environment of single sideband HF operations. This digital communications mode encodes messages by rapidly shifting the phase of an audio signal waveform between two states to form sequences of binary character codes. The two waveform phase states serve the same function as two different tones or on/off transmission states. The PSK31 tone sounds like a whining whistle, and a sound card interface connects the computer and radio so that software may control the transmission and reception of PSK31 signals. PSK31 uses a very narrow bandwidth and is effective for QRP (low power) transmissions. PSK31 has become a very popular mode in recent years!

Sound Card Interface (SCI): When conducting digital communications using a computer, the sound card provides audio to the microphone input (during transmission) and converts received audio to digital form for computer processing of messages. Essentially, the sound card interface translates between audio signals used by the radio and digital signals used by the computer. A sound card interface is prudent, but not absolutely required, for PSK31 operations.

T4A07

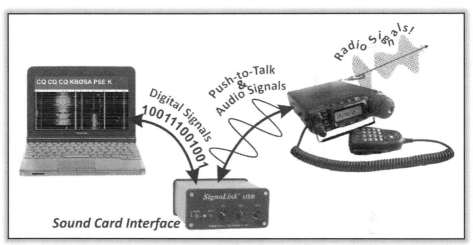

Figure 10.2: PSK31 Sound Card Interface Functionality

MFSK: *Multiple Frequency Shift Keying* is a digital communications method that uses more than two audio frequencies to encode text or data characters. The transmission of MFSK is often very musical as the sequence of tones alternate rapidly. There are many different MFSK forms including MFSK16 (16 tones), Olivia, Thor, and others. MFSK uses more bandwidth than PSK systems (like PSK31), but is often more robust in noisy conditions.

Automatic Packet Reporting System (APRS) is a digital mode that **can send automatic position reports from a mobile amateur radio station using data provided by a Global Positioning System receiver** (GPS receiver). Position coordinate information (and other digital packet information) is transmitted via *digipeaters*, or digital repeaters, that relay packets to

T8D02 T8D03

a receiving network or internet gateway. Like phone repeaters, **APRS network digipeaters operate under automatic control** to forward packet signals.

Figure 10.3: HT with Built-In GPS and TNC

One application of APRS is to provide real time tactical digital communications in conjunction with a map showing the location of stations. Such a mapping function can be affected in a locally implemented computer network or, when received by an internet gateway, station position reports may be posted on a web server map that is publicly accessible, such as the APRS.fi web site.

Other APRS data reports may include short messages, weather reports, telemetry data, or radio direction finding bearings. Some radios are sold with built-in GPS receivers and APRS capability, while other radios must be interfaced to a separate GPS receiver via a terminal node controller.

Internet Radio Linking Project (IRLP): IRLP is a technique to connect amateur radio systems, such as repeaters, via the Internet using Voice Over Internet Protocol (VoIP). **VoIP is a method of delivering voice communications over the Internet using digital techniques.** Two repeaters may be joined so that all transmissions received and repeated locally by either station are also repeated by the other station in a different geographic location. That is, each station not only transmits RF locally, but also sends a digitally converted VoIP signal through the Internet to the other repeater where reconversion to RF signals occurs and an identical transmission is made from the linked repeater station.

Gateway: The name given to an amateur radio station that is used to connect other amateur stations to the Internet is a gateway. Thus, an IRLP repeater station is a gateway station. Two major linking systems use VoIP: IRLP and Echolink. While these two systems operate similarly, there are some differences. Echolink allows amateur operators to use a personal computer as an Echolink gateway, connecting the computer with microphone and audio capability to any other Echolink node, whether that node is a computer or a repeater gateway station.

Specifying IRLP Nodes: When using a portable transceiver to connect an IRLP gateway, you may select a specific IRLP node

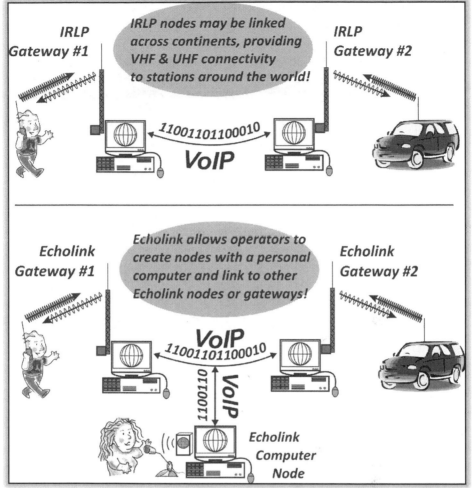

Figure 10.4: IRLP and Echolink VoIP Operational Relationships

using the keypad to transmit the IRLP node ID. Such **access to an IRLP node is accomplished with DTMF tones.** DTMF tones are like those transmitted over telephone when you tone dial a telephone number.

Repeater Directory: A list of active nodes that use VoIP may be obtained from a repeater directory. A repeater directory can be obtained in book form from most ham radio distributors, and IRLP or Echolink listings may also be found through an Internet search.

Other Digital Modes: Some radio manufacturers have implemented highly capable digital modes unique to their radio brand. The Icom D-Star digital voice (DV) mode is one popular example. Voice audio is digitized to be transmitted and received as a digital RF stream of data, eliminating any RF analog signal in transmitting and receiving. A network of voice and data digital repeaters supports worldwide communications with digital voice and data.

Errors in Digital Transmissions: Because digital transmission rely upon series of discrete signals, it is somewhat easy for a packet of digits to be incorrectly interpreted if only one of the hundreds or thousands of digits transmitted is omitted or incorrectly decoded. **Any of the following error checking methods may be included in a packet transmission** to help insure correct receipt:

T8D08

Figure 10.3a: HT with DV capability and GPS data. Icom ID-31A

Check Sum: A value **included in a packet transmission to permit error detection,** the check sum is a mathematical tool for checking the integrity of the data transmission. Essentially, the received check sum in the packet must match a calculated summation of the data bits received in order for the digital packet to be confirmed valid and error free.

Header: Data **included in a packet transmission** at the beginning of a packet that **may include the call sign of the station to which the information is being sent,** time stamp, IP address, check sum, sending station ID or call sign, and other information.

T8D11

Automatic Repeat Request (ARQ): Included in a packet transmission in case of error, this is a digital scheme whereby the receiving station detects errors and sends a request to the sending station to retransmit the information.

T3A10

BER: The *Bit Error Rate* is a count of the number of omitted or altered data bits in a reception due to noise, interference, distortion, or faulty synchronization. **Error rates are likely to increase if VHF or UHF data signals propagate over multiple paths,** thereby arriving at the receiving station with slightly different time or phase and causing multipath interference, as discussed for phone mode in Section 1.2, *Ham Communication Basics*.

Radio Remote Control: Radio control of model vehicles such as airplanes, or other receiving devices, commonly use digital signals. Two main FCC rules apply to radio remote control activities:

Maximum Power allowed when transmitting telecommand signals to radio controlled models is 1 Watt. `T8C07`

Identification: **When sending signals to a radio control model using amateur frequencies a label affixed to the transmitter indicating the licensee's name, call sign, and address is required in place of on-air identification. Transmitting signals to control a model craft is the only circumstance an amateur station may transmit without identifying** by call sign. `T8C08` `T1D11`

Amateur Television: Although not really a digital mode, television transmissions with amateur radio utilize unique data transmission formats and the equipment frequently involves a computer interface for the video source. Two basic amateur TV signal types are *slow-scan television* (SSTV) and *fast-scan television* (FSTV).

Slow-scan TV: SSTV uses only about 3 kHz of bandwidth, similar to SSB phone mode. Thus, it can be transmitted on the HF bands. However, a single frame image typically requires several seconds to a couple of minutes to transmit. As such, SSTV is not terrific at depicting motion so much as providing interval "snapshots in time" of the scene your camera is capturing.

Fast-scan TV: FSTV is nearly identical in quality to broadcast television because it utilizes the same transmission standard as commercial broadcasting and because it uses much greater bandwidth than SSTV. The lowest frequency practical for FSTV due to bandwidth considerations is the UHF 70 cm band. **The typical bandwidth of analog FSTV transmissions on the 70 cm band is about 6 MHz.** With this bandwidth `T8A10` FSTV can produce broadcast quality video and sound. **Analog fast-scan color TV signals utilize a type of transmission indicated by the term *NTSC*,** which is a TV transmission format standard established `T8D04` by the *National Television System Committee*.

With a video camera, a computer, and amateur TV software, you can get started experimenting with amateur television as a new Technician!

In spite of some of the technical methods used to make digital modes come to life, implementing them with your radio is really very easy. For most digital modes just a software installation and perhaps an electronic box connected between radio and computer will get you started in the world of digital communications over the amateur bands. No need to fear computers at all, especially in the ham shack. Try the Technician question pool items for **Section 10.0**, then come back for a journey into the final frontier!

www.HamRadioSchool.com/tech_media

Summary Table of Digital Modes and Characteristics

Digital Mode	Description	Hardware/Comments
CW	Uses International Morse Code	Use Straight Key, Electronic Keyer, or Computer Keyboard
Packet	Transmits email, APRS data, text messages	Terminal Node Controller (TNC) between radio & computer
APRS	Automatic Packet Reporting System	Uses GPS receiver; location mapping; automatic digipeaters
PSK31	Phase Shift Keying; Low data transmission rate mode	Sound card interface; computer; keyboard-to-keyboard messaging
IRLP & Echolink	Uses VoIP internet link called "gateway"	Use keypad DTMF tones to transmit IRLP node ID for linking systems together
MFSK	Multiple audio tones encode information	Sound card interface; computer
FSTV	Fast-scan television	NTSC signal, 6 MHz bandwidth, on 70cm band (or higher freq.)
Radio Remote Control	For model airplanes, vehicles, rockets, etc.	1 watt max power; call sign label on transmitter instead of on-air ID

11.0   Space Contacts

❝ *That's one small step for a ham, one giant leap for hamkind. – Anonymous*

With your Technician license, a handheld 2m/70cm transceiver, and a directional antenna, you can make long distance contacts using orbital satellites as repeaters and you can even talk to astronauts on the International Space Station! Let's learn how to take this small step.

Space Station: By FCC Part 97 definition, a space station is an amateur station located more than 50 km above the earth's surface. Multiple amateur radio satellites reside in *low earth orbit* (LEO) that are essentially repeaters in space.

As one of these amateur radio satellites passes over your position you can talk to amateur radio operators in other countries, or stations hundreds of miles away, via the satellite-based repeater that will relay your UHF/ VHF signals across a wide area. You may also be able to contact amateur operator astronauts onboard the International Space Station (ISS). Using a handheld beam antenna with your HT you can manually track the satellite across the sky and get very good results with 5 watts of power or less!

Figure 11.1: Early Morning ISS Contact

Orbit and Path: Amateur satellites may be in one of several different types of orbits, or maneuvers about the earth in circular or elliptical paths.

LEO is low earth orbit, meaning that a satellite or space station is orbiting up to a few hundred miles above the earth. (This may be compared to a geostationary orbit in which a satellite is about 22,800 miles above the earth's equator such that it orbits once per 24 hours, thereby remaining over one position on the earth's surface. Amateur radio satellites are not usually lifted into geostationary orbits.)

Polar Orbit: LEO amateur radio satellites will commonly be placed in *polar orbits* in which the satellite passes over or near the north and south geographic poles of the earth. In this way the satellite will pass within contact range of virtually every position on earth over the course of several orbits, as the earth turns beneath it. If the satellite is moving south-to-north over your position it is said to have an *ascending approach* or orbit. If it is moving north-to-south, it is said to have a *descending approach* or orbit.

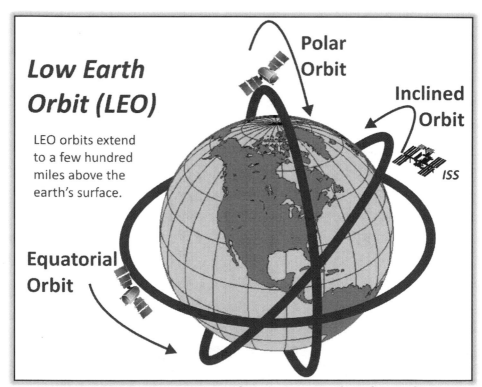

Figure 11.2: Comparison of Basic Low Earth Orbit Paths

Contact Time: The duration of a satellite's pass over your location will depend significantly upon its height above the horizon. Passes near the horizon will result in brief contact periods. Passes directly overhead will provide the longest contact periods, typically up to several minutes as the satellite moves from horizon to horizon.

Because the satellite window is brief, and because its coverage may extend over an area of hundreds of thousands of square miles, satellite contacts must be conducted with great efficiency. Many operators may be attempting to use the satellite simultaneously, and usually there is only one repeater frequency pair available. Most contacts will consist simply of call sign and grid square location exchanges.

Satellite Tracking Program: To determine the time period during which an amateur satellite or space station can be accessed you may use a satellite tracking program with your personal computer. **Such programs use the satellite's Keplerian elements as input,** along with the correct time and your station location to calculate the time and precise path of a satellite pass overhead. The Keplerian elements mathematically define a satellite's orbit. `T8B06`

Tracking programs, multiple internet sites, and even mobile device apps provide regularly updated satellite orbit information. With many of these resources you can simply identify your location by postal zip code, by grid square locator, or by latitude-longitude coordinate and obtain a customized report of upcoming satellite passes within your horizon. These customized reports and **tracking programs will provide maps showing real time position of the satellite track over the earth,** as well as **the time, azimuth and elevation of start, maximum altitude, and end of pass. The apparent frequency of the satellite transmission, including effects of Doppler shift,** may also be included in a report. (See forward paragraph on Doppler shift, this section.) With all of this information you can readily track the bird's path across your local sky. See Figure 11.3, next page. `T8B03`

Uplink / Downlink: The *uplink frequency* is the frequency used to transmit to the satellite. The *downlink frequency* is the frequency used to receive the satellite's transmissions.

Split Channel: Commonly a *split channel* arrangement – a UHF and a VHF frequency pair or *duplex* channel – will be used for the satellite uplink/downlink pair. This is much like a normal repeater offset in which your radio automatically shifts to the transmit frequency when you PTT, only in this case the offset is between two different bands, the 2m (VHF) and 70cm (UHF) bands. Refer to your radio user's manual for setting up a split

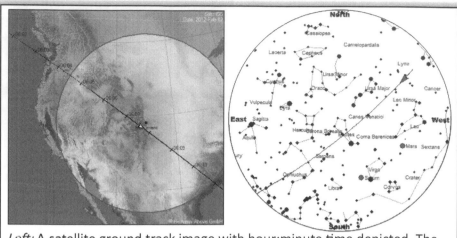

Left: A satellite ground track image with hour:minute time depicted. The circle indicates the position where the satellite will be 10 degrees above the horizon for the user-selected observation position on earth.

Right: A star chart indicating the path of the selected satellite pass relative to constellations, planets, and the moon. *Courtesy of Heavens-Above.com*

Figure 11.3: Example Online Satellite Tracking Products

frequency or duplex channel, sometimes called an "*odd split.*" You should note the satellite mode to find the specific frequency split arrangement for a given satellite. (Note: The ISS also tends to use split channel operations for phone contacts with astronaut amateurs.)

Mode: The uplink / downlink frequency split arrangement is referred to as the satellite *mode*. (This should not be confused with earthbound transmission modes that instead refer to the method of modulating the signal, such as FM, SSB, or CW.) For example, **if the satellite is said to be operating in "mode U/V," this means that the satellite uplink is in the 70cm band (UHF) and the downlink is in the 2m band (VHF).** Hence, "U/V." Mode "V/U" would be the opposite, where uplink is on 2m band and downlink is on 70cm band.

FM Packet: A commonly used method of sending signals to and from a digital satellite is FM Packet. This method sends bursts, or *packets*, of digital information via UHF/VHF FM modulation to a satellite. The digital satellite may immediately repeat the packet or store it for transmission later during a pass over another geographical area designated by the sender.

T8B08

T8B11

License Privileges: Any amateur whose license privileges allow them to transmit on the satellite uplink frequency may be the control operator of a station communicating through an amateur satellite or space station. Most satellites and the ISS use UHF and VHF amateur frequencies. **Any amateur holding a Technician or higher class license may make contact with an amateur station on the International Space Station using 2 meter and 70 cm band amateur radio frequencies.**

Power Requirements: Like any amateur communication, **the transmitter power used on the uplink frequency of an amateur satellite or space station should be the minimum amount of power needed to complete the contact.** Usually you will need no more than the typical 5W of a modern HT radio, coupled with an appropriate directional antenna pointed at the satellite, to make reliable contacts.

Telecommand: By FCC Part 97 definition, a telecommand is a one-way transmission to initiate, modify or terminate functions of a device at a distance. Amateur satellite controllers must use telecommands sent from earth to the satellite station to operate the satellite station. Controllers of earthbound repeater stations may also use telecommands to change remote repeater station functions, especially if the repeater is located in a difficult to reach area, such as a mountain top.

Telemetry: By FCC Part 97 definition, telemetry is a one-way transmission of measurements at a distance from the measuring instrument. A satellite may transmit measurements of its own condition, such as a power status measurement, as telemetry back to a ground station.

Satellite Beacon: A satellite may transmit information from space containing information about the satellite in its beacon. Often, this telemetry is transmitted on a unique frequency from the satellite, and in some cases the beacon may be briefly activated by telecommand when the satellite controller (or another amateur operator) wishes to receive the beacon telemetry.

Common Transmission Effects: Due to the motion of satellites and space stations, you may experience some unique audio effects with space contacts that are not typical of other amateur communications.

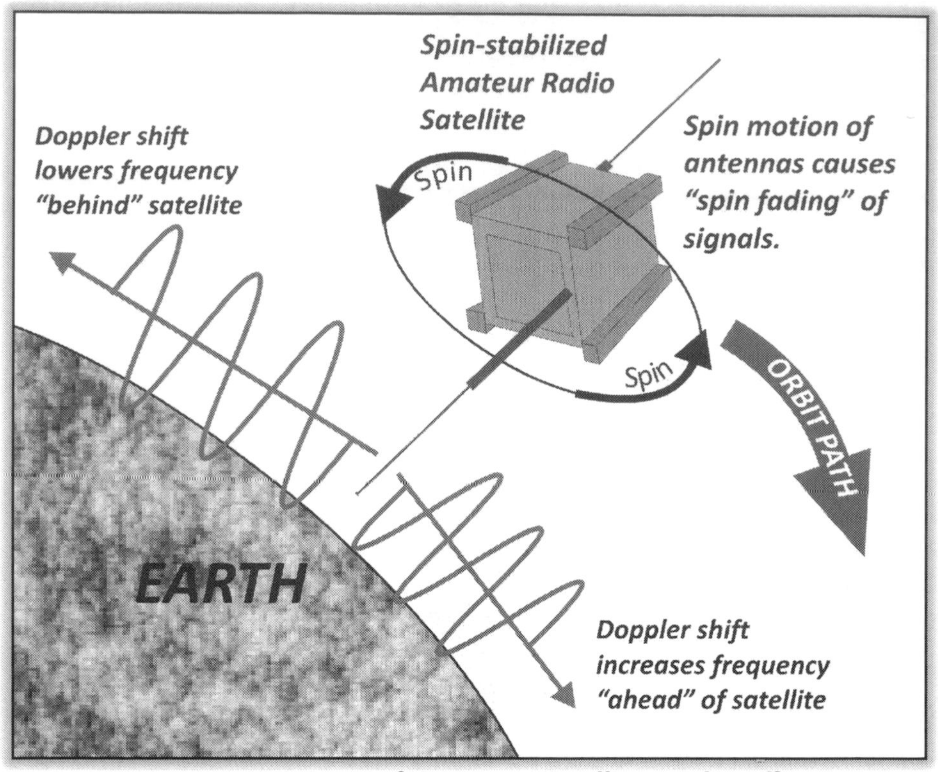

Figure 11.4: Causes of Common Satellite Audio Effects

Spin Fading: Satellites are often rotating to provide stability. **Rotation of the satellite and its antennas causes spin fading of satellite signals,** which is a fluctuation of signal strength or quality as the satellite spins and its antenna polarization changes with the spin.

Doppler Shift: An observed change in signal frequency caused by relative motion between the satellite and the earth station is Doppler Shift. You will notice Doppler Shift as a gradual change in the tone of satellite signals, from higher to lower tone, because the satellite is moving fast enough to cause minor compression of RF frequencies as it approaches your position, and minor rarefaction (lowering) of RF frequencies as it moves away from your position. This is the same effect with sound waves that causes a swiftly passing train's whistle or horn to sound higher pitched as it approaches and shift to a lower pitch as it passes by and moves away. Usually with FM ops this does not disrupt communications, and it can be alleviated with minor receiver tuning changes over the period of the satellite pass, if desired. With SSB mode, Doppler effects are much more significant, requiring tuning changes during the pass.

Amateur radio satellites really are a giant leap for hams. Getting VHF and UHF signals spread across such a vast area is a rare treat, and satellite contacts are really fun. And while the crew of the International Space Station has had sporadic activity with amateur operators onboard over the years, making contact with another human being in space is a delight I guarantee you will never forget!

We are approaching the final frontier of our initial amateur radio expedition! Only a couple more topics to blast off into. Beat up the **Section 11.0** Technician questions on Space Contacts and we'll take a look at issues of radio interference.

www.HamRadioSchool.com/tech_media

Figure 11.5: ISS Commander Doug Wheelock, KF5BOC

Courtesy NASA/JPL-Caltech

Astronaut Douglas Wheelock, Colonel, US Army, was very active on amateur radio from orbit during his long-duration stay aboard the International Space Station, June - November 2010. Numerous earthly hams were thrilled to make contact with him, collecting a rare and coveted prize in amateur radio. The author and his son, WØJAK, were each lucky to make contact with Colonel Wheelock on the morning of October 13, 2010, using an HT radio and a dual-band handheld Yagi antenna, as shown in Figure 11.1. Thank you, sir!

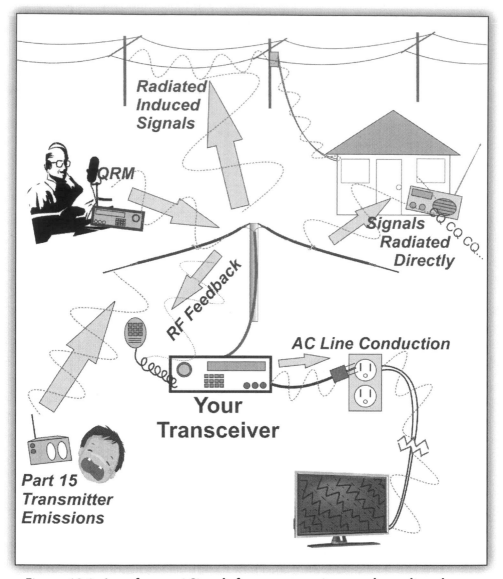

Figure 12.0: Interference! Signals from your station may be radiated directly to other devices or conducted along AC power lines to other devices. Radiated signals may induce currents on cables or wires to be conducted into other devices. Your radio may even inadvertently receive its own signal transmissions via the microphone cord behaving like an antenna. Other amateur radio station transmissions on nearby or overlapping frequencies may interfere with your communications, and non-licensed emitters such as Part 15 devices may cause noise on your received audio. Good amateur practice and common filtering techniques can reduce or eliminate most interference problems. Let's see how...

12.0 Avoiding Interference

❝ The radio makes hideous sounds. – Bob Dylan

Interference happens. Sometimes your radio will indeed make hideous sounds due to the effects of other radio stations or transmitters. Your radio may impose some hideous sounds or images of its own on other electronic devices as well. As a licensed amateur radio operator it is your responsibility to have familiarity with the FCC regulations regarding interference and with the common methods of resolving interference when it rears its hideous head. Nobody wants an ongoing argument with a neighbor over a few flying frequencies. Keep it cool with the following good information.

Interference is the undesirable reception of RF signals produced either properly or improperly by another electronic device. Interference may be received by your radio station from other sources, or interference may be produced by your radio station and affect other devices. Usually, interference problems can be easily solved with one or more standard approaches. Filtering at the offended or receiving device is the most common resolution approach. Let's first consider the case of your ham radio transmissions causing interference with other devices.

Ham Interference to Other Devices: Your station transmissions may interfere with other electronic devices, including other radio receivers and devices never intended to receive radio signals at all. Your RF signals may travel from your transmitter to other devices by two different ways, and possibly both ways simultaneously:

Radiated Signals: The wires associated with other devices can act as antennas to inadvertently receive your station's radiated signals. Wiring such as power cords, speaker wires, TV antennas and cables, component connecting cables, or even internal wiring within electronic devices may pick up your RF signals.

Conducted Signals: In addition to radiating RF via your station antenna, your transmitter may also output signals onto household AC wiring, or such wiring may have RF signals induced on it, and these signals are conducted into other powered equipment to impose interference.

We'll consider some simple methods of filtering these signals out of the other devices in a moment, but first let's take note of some troublesome types of **RF emissions that may cause radio frequency interference: Fundamental overload, spurious emissions (including harmonics),** and RF feedback into your transmitter.

Fundamental Overload: Interference in a radio receiver caused by very strong signals. You may experience fundamental overload with your station if another station is transmitting a strong signal very nearby, especially in the same band. With fundamental overload the receiver fails to reject these undesired signals that overload the receiver circuitry and may cause distorted, unintelligible audio, and override any other weaker signals you may desire to receive. Your station may cause fundamental overload of a telephone, television, or commercial radio receiver if you are transmitting very strong signals. For instance, **a broadcast AM or FM radio may receive an amateur radio transmission unintentionally because the receiver is unable to reject strong signals outside the AM or FM band.**

Spurious Emissions: Undesired radio frequency emissions not deliberately transmitted by a radio transmitter are called spurious emissions. A spurious emission is any radio frequency transmission outside of the intended and assigned bandwidth for the operating mode being used. Two of the more common types of spurious emissions are harmonics and splatter.

Harmonics: Emissions that are frequency multiples of the intended (or 'fundamental') frequency of a transmitter are called harmonics. Virtually all transmitters produce some harmonics at low power levels. [Typically the 2nd harmonic (double the fundamental frequency) or 3rd harmonic (triple the fundamental) are the strongest harmonic frequencies, but other multiples may also cause interference with devices.] Harmonics generated by your station may lie outside of the amateur bands and cause interference in non-amateur radio receivers and electronic devices. Harmonics are one type of spurious emission, as depicted in Figure 12.1.

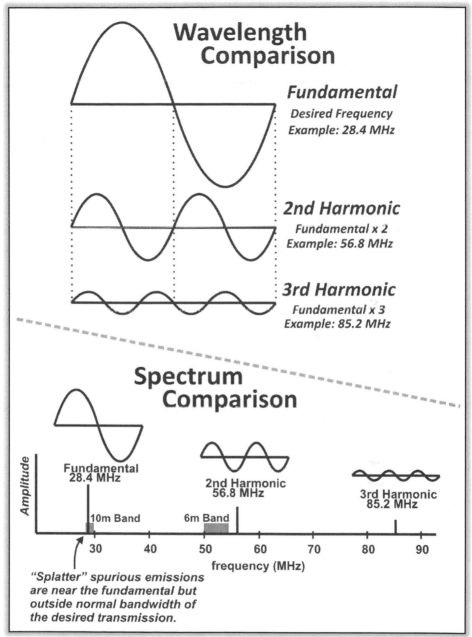

Figure 12.1: Spurious Emissions - Harmonics and Splatter

Splatter: Transmissions of excessive bandwidth. For instance, if your SSB transmitter is emitting 20 kHz worth of frequencies, you are emitting about 17 kHz of spurious emissions outside of the necessary and proper 3 kHz bandwidth for SSB mode. Splatter will not make friends on the air. Check your transmitter for off-frequency operation or spurious emissions if you receive a report that your station's transmissions are causing splatter or interference with nearby frequencies!

RF Feedback: A garbled, distorted, or unintelligible transmission is a symptom of RF feedback. This is caused by your own transmitted signal being fed back into your transmitter unintentionally. For example, if your microphone and its cable act as an effective antenna for the frequency on which you are operating, your signal will be fed back into your transmitter. RF feedback can usually be alleviated by increasing the separation of the transmitter and antenna, or by adding a simple filter to the microphone cable. (See ferrite choke, below.)

Alleviating Interference with Filters: No matter the specific type of RF emissions causing interference to another device, easy-to-implement and in-expensive filters placed on the receiving device will usually work to reduce or eliminate the interference caused by your station. **Snap-on ferrite chokes, low-pass and high-pass filters, band-reject and band-pass filters may all be useful in correcting a radio frequency interference problem.** When an interference problem arises with a neighbor, a combination of cordial communication, polite investigation, and sound technical fixes usually helps maintain friendships and the enjoyment of amateur radio. Let's explore a few common types of friendship-saving filters.

> **Ferrite Choke:** One of the simplest and cheapest filtering solutions for audio devices is the ferrite or magnetic choke (also known as snap-on chokes). A ferrite choke will reduce RF current flowing on the shield of an audio cable (the cable being an "inadvertent receiver" antenna). Assist your neighbor in snapping one or two ferrite chokes on audio cables such as speaker lines to help avoid destroying his music listening enjoyment with your ham radio transmissions. Additionally, **distorted audio caused by RF current flowing on the shield of a microphone cable may be cured using a ferrite choke.**

> **RF Filters:** A type of low-pass filter, RF filters allow lower frequency signals such as audio signals to pass, while blocking higher frequencies such as RF. **Interference by an amateur transmitter to a nearby telephone can be reduced or eliminated by putting an RF filter on the telephone.** These filters are readily available as small plug-and-forget modules that fit into standard telephone jacks. If you hear your radio transmissions through the phone, try one of these inexpensive modules first.

Other RF filters are designed to pass and block specific frequency ranges. Low-pass or high-pass filters allow the passing of frequencies above (high-pass) or below (low-pass) a specific frequency value, while blocking all others. A band-pass filter allows a range of specified frequencies to pass (the band), while blocking all frequencies above and below the pass band. The inverse type of filter is called a band-reject filter, blocking a specified band of frequencies while allowing all others to pass. Although sometimes requiring careful consideration, these types of filters interfered devices may be purchased or created to solve almost any type of RF interference. For example, **overload of a non-amateur radio or TV receiver by an amateur signal may be reduced or eliminated with a filter at the antenna input of the affected receiver, blocking the amateur signal** while allowing desired signals to pass.

Harmonic Filtering of Transmitter: A very common filtering method used on most modern transmitters addresses the harmonics spurious emission described earlier in this section. **A filter installed between the transmitter and the antenna can reduce harmonic emissions from**

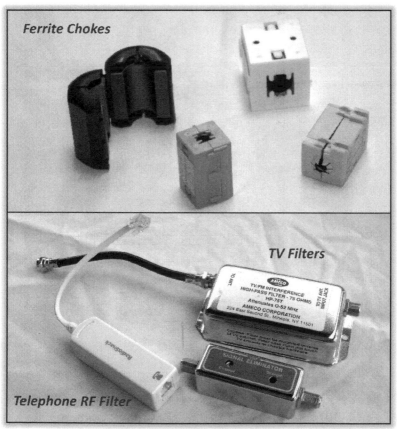

Figure 12.2: Examples of Chokes and Filters

your station. Many modern transceivers have harmonic filters installed as standard components.

Non-filtering Considerations: Before jumping to a filter fix, it's a good idea to check some other basic things first. For instance, poor connectors on interfered device cables can sometimes promote interference. **The first step to resolving cable TV interference from your ham radio transmissions might be to ensure all TV coaxial connectors are installed properly.** You can also conduct some other simple investigations: **If a neighbor tells you that your station's transmissions are interfering with their radio or TV reception, make sure that your station is functioning properly and that it does not cause interference to your own radio or television when it is tuned to the same channel** as your neighbor's device.

Other Device Interference to Ham Stations: Sometimes other devices, either intentional or unintentional emitters, may cause interference to your station. You will usually hear this type of interference in your receive audio. The source of the interference could be from a nearby faulty power line, from an electric motor or other device, or from another electronic device that emits RF intentionally. It could even be from intentional jamming of RF signals. Often, the nature of the noise will be a sufficient clue to the source of the interference. It may be necessary in some cases to track down the source of interference using radio direction finding.

Radio direction finding is a method used to locate sources of noise interference or jamming. A simple directional antenna on a mobile receiver such as an HT radio is often sufficient to track down troublesome sources of interference such as electrical noise. The S-meter of the receiver may be a sufficient index to get a fix on an offending RF source, as it will show increased signal strength as the directional antenna is pointed in the direction of the RF source.

Interference from Neighbors: If something in a neighbor's home is causing harmful interference to your amateur station, you should:

1. **Work with your neighbor to identify the offending device.**
2. **Politely inform your neighbor about the rules that prohibit the use of devices which cause interference.**
3. **Check your station and make sure it meets the standards of good amateur practice.**

Part 15 Devices: Many modern household electronic devices are intentional transmitters: Baby monitors, remotely controlled toys, wireless computer routers, cordless phones, and many others. Most of these are classified by the FCC as a **Part 15 device, an unlicensed device that may emit low powered radio signals on frequencies used by a licensed service.** It is possible for Part 15 devices to cause interference with your station, and operators of such devices are required to avoid use that imposes such interference. Still, common courtesy and polite negotiation should be the approach should someone else's device be a source of trouble.

T7B09

Mobile Station Interference Problems: Mobile stations in automobiles require some specific implementations to avoid interference from an automobile's electrical systems.

Alternator Whine: The source of a high-pitched whine that varies with engine speed in a mobile transceiver's receive audio is the alternator. The car's alternator generates AC power and produces this broadband interference. **If another operator reports a variable high-pitched whine on the audio from your mobile transmitter, noise from the vehicle's electrical system is being transmitted along with your speech audio.** Usually, alleviating transmitted electrical system noise will require a suppression technique applied to the offending vehicle source, such as spark plug suppressors or repair or replacement of the alternator or computer controller module generating the noise.

T4A10

T4A12

Noise Blanker: Turning on the radio's noise blanker can help reduce ignition interference to the receiver. The noise blanker is a special type of filter designed to reduce broadband noise of a regular frequency or pulse, like that created by the engine's electric ignition system. Most modern radios will have a noise blanker filtering option available in the setup menu structure. The noise blanker effects only the receive audio and will not alleviate transmitted electrical system noise from your mobile station.

T4B05

Battery Connections: A mobile transceiver's power cable negative return connection should be made at the battery or engine block ground strap. Using direct and dedicated power connections from the car battery, with in-line fuses and avoiding all use of any automobile wiring, will help avoid electrical system interference and potential electrical hazards.

T4A11

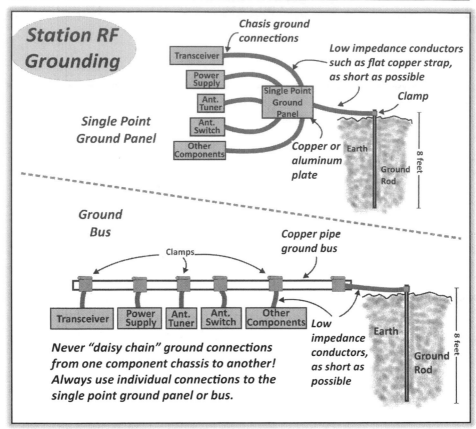

Figure 12.3: Station Single Point Grounding Options

Grounding: Grounding your mobile radio to the automobile chassis may help reduce ground loop interference. Grounding your base station to conductive rods driven into the earth may help alleviate the same type of undesirable currents. *Ground loop* currents are caused by variations in the ground voltage level among different components of a radio station. A single-point ground connection, as illustrated in Figures 12.3 and 12.4, is best to eliminate ground loop currents. **Use of a flat strap conductor is best for RF grounding,** such as wide copper strap, since it offers greater surface area on which RF currents flow, minimizing the resistance of RF currents flowing to ground.

T4A08

Rejecting QRM: *QRM*, or interference from other amateur stations transmitting on nearby frequencies, may be rejected by varying your radio's receive filter, if available. **Having multiple receive bandwidth choices on a multimode transceiver is an advantage that permits noise or inter-**

T4B08

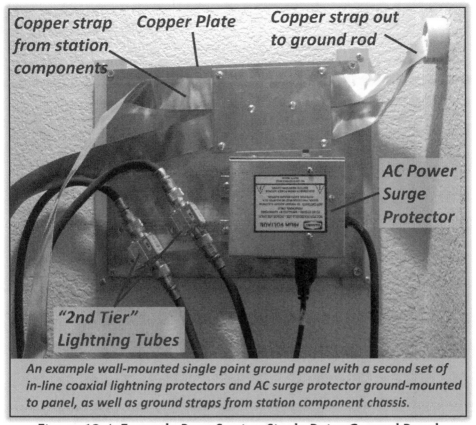

Copper strap from station components

Copper Plate

Copper strap out to ground rod

AC Power Surge Protector

"2nd Tier" Lightning Tubes

An example wall-mounted single point ground panel with a second set of in-line coaxial lightning protectors and AC surge protector ground-mounted to panel, as well as ground straps from station component chassis.

Figure 12.4: Example Base Station Single Point Ground Panel

ference reduction by selecting a bandwidth matching the mode.
That is, you may select a filter that passes only enough RF bandwidth for the mode you are using and rejects frequencies outside that mode's normal bandwidth. [Review mode bandwidths in section 6.3, *How Radio Works.*]

Selectivity: The term that describes the ability of a receiver to discriminate between multiple signals is selectivity. Your selected receive filter bandwidth is one factor that determines your receiver's selectivity. Other factors, such as the intermediate frequency conversion system, will also affect selectivity. Selectivity is an important metric defining the quality of a receiver. [T7A04]

SSB Filtering: For single sideband mode an appropriate receive filter to select to minimize interference is 2400 Hz (2.4 kHz). Since a typical SSB signal may be up to 3000 Hz (3.0 kHz) wide, this filter selection will reject noise or QRM on adjacent frequencies while allowing [T4B09]

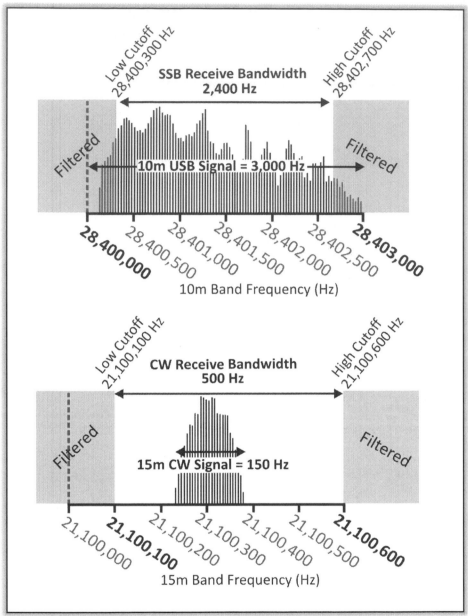

Figure 12.5: Matching Filters to Bandwidth for QRM Rejection

sufficient bandwidth for good audio to pass through to your receiver. This scenario is illustrated in Figure 12.5 with a 10m band example.

T4B10

CW Filtering: For CW reception an appropriate receive filter to select to minimize noise and interference is 500 Hz. A typical CW signal may be about 150 Hz wide, but filters narrower than 500

| High & Low Cutoff Adjustment Controls | Graphic Receive Bandwidth Scale | Low Cutoff Frequency Index | High Cutoff Frequency Index |

Figure 12.6: Example of HF Station Filter Bandwidth Selection

Hz are less common. A 500 Hz filter is usually sufficient to reject adjacent frequency noise or QRM and isolate the desired CW signal. (This filter is also suitable for PSK31 mode, as the signal bandwidth is about 300 Hz.) A CW example is illustrated in the lower part of Figure 12.5.

Filtering Other Modes: Similarly for other modes (PSK31, AM, various digital modes), select a filter that matches the bandwidth of the mode in order to best reject noise and interference on nearby frequencies. Many modern radios provide convenient operator manipulation of filter bandwidths by digital signal processing and other methods.

Figure 12.6 depicts one base station filter selection example. The high and low cutoff frequencies of the desired receive band are adjusted with two rotary knobs at the lower left. The audio band corresponding index values for the cutoff frequencies are displayed as "LOCUT" and "HICUT." The resulting receive bandwidth is graphically displayed by a curved line scale that lengthens or shortens with receive bandwidth. Independent adjustment of the low cutoff and high cutoff frequencies allows easy operator control of the bandwidth and positioning of the receive band in order that QRM or other interference may be rejected.

Dealing with interference promptly and correctly is much easier than dealing with irate neighbors, irate amateur operators, or hideous sounds. You may notice some fundamental overload when operating in close proximity to other stations with your FM HT radio or mobile station, and you'll surely get QRM to reject once you get started with the 10 meter band using SSB mode. You might even discover that you have some offending emissions coming from sources in or near your home creating noise on your SSB receiver. These can be frustrating at times. The best policy as a new ham when faced with a vexing interference problem is to remain calm and seek the sage advice of an experienced ham, or "Elmer," who is eager to help. Together you will usually be able to reduce or eliminate the interference problem.

Don't forget to practice the questions from the pool for Avoiding Interference, **Section 12.0**!

www.HamRadioSchool.com/tech_media

13.0   Safety

❝ *I could tell that my parents hated me. My bath toys were a toaster and a radio. – Rodney Dangerfield*

Most ham radio operations and station installation activities are not quite as hazardous as Rodney's childhood radio experience. And most ham shacks do not include toasters at all. However, because stations that are more elaborate than an HT will require some electrical power connections, will perhaps involve exterior antennas and towers, and typically will provide higher RF power transmission, safety becomes paramount. In this chapter we will examine potential hazards and safe practices that can help you avoid injury or equipment damage.

In Section 13.1 we will address basic electrical safety. It is important that you understand the sources of electrical shock associated with your station, as well as practical precautions for avoiding it. You should also be aware of hazards that batteries present and know how to safely charge, discharge, and store your batteries.

Section 13.2 highlights common sense precautions to take when erecting and operating tall antennas and towers. From proper climbing gear to grounding for lightning strikes, you will learn how to stay alive and uninjured to transmit another day.

Exposure to radio frequency emissions is the subject of Section 13.3. As an amateur station operator you should be able to estimate the RF exposure to humans that your station imposes, and you should know how to take action to reduce exposure levels when warranted by exposure guidelines.

Let's examine these common sense measures for keeping ourselves, our friends and neighbors, and our families safe while we enjoy amateur radio.

13.1 Safety — Electrical Safety

Electrical Safety involves avoiding electrical shock through knowledge of potential dangers and taking proper precautions.

Dangerous Electric Shock: The commonly accepted value for the lowest voltage that can cause a dangerous electric shock is about 30 volts, but it is the electrical *current* that flows and causes health hazards. **Current flowing through the body causes health hazards by:**

- **Heating tissue** (burns)
- **Disrupting the electrical functions of cells** (nervous system disfunction or loss of consciousness)
- **Causing involuntary muscle contractions** (including stopping the heart and inability to control body movements)

Typical household AC voltage of 120 volts is more than enough to be deadly. Even 12v batteries, such as high capacity lead-acid cells, can provide fatal currents especially when multiple cells are connected in series such that higher voltages result. Be very careful that you do not come into contact with bare wires connected to power sources or with unprotected battery terminals that may send a surge of current through your body. Also, because currents passing through your body are seeking a path to electrical ground, it is a good idea to always wear shoes so that some insulation between you and earth ground is afforded. Your bare feet will provide a low resistance pathway directly to ground. It pays to be conscientious around any source of current, regardless of voltage levels.

Sources of Electric Shock: Power supplies, even when turned off and disconnected, may still present a hazard of electric shock from stored charge in large capacitors. Allow ample time for capacitors to discharge before touching any part of the circuits. It is also feasible to carefully discharge capacitors through resistors, safely dissipating the energy into heat, if the circuit has been constructed with such a safety feature. If you are not sure, take no chances. Any equipment while powered from 120 V AC circuits presents a significant hazard. Batteries, while usually below 30 V, may still deliver a painful and dangerous shock.

T0A02

T0A11

Electrical Precautions: **Guard against electrical shock at your station by:**

- **Using three-wire cords and plugs for all AC powered equipment**
- **Connecting all AC powered station equipment to a common safety ground**
- **Using a circuit protected ground-fault interrupter (GFI electrical outlet)**
- **Placing a fuse or circuit breaker in series with the AC "hot" conductor on any home-built equipment powered from 120V AC circuits**

Safety Ground: **The green wire in a three-wire electrical AC plug is connected to the safety ground.** *Green to ground!* The safety ground helps shunt any stray current to ground, reducing the risk of electrical shock and overloads in circuits.

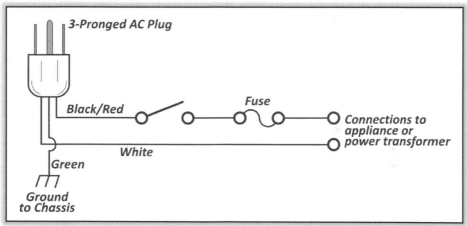

Figure 13.1: Wiring Diagram of Common 3-Pronged AC Plug

Fuses: **In an electrical circuit fuses interrupt power in case of over-load** and help prevent electrical shock and fire hazards. **Never install a higher ampere rated fuse than is called for in a circuit or excessive current could cause a fire.** The whole purpose of a fuse is to break and disconnect the circuit any time excessive current is drawn through the wire by accident. If the fuse is not in place or if it is rated too high, excessive current will heat the wires, possibly melting insulation, burning or shocking you, and possibly starting a fire. Fuses are cheap. Fires and funeral are expensive. Use fuses.

Figure 13.2: In-line Fuses in a Radio Power Cable

Batteries may cause painful shock and present additional hazards when charging or discharging. When recharging a battery, take all precautions and ensure the procedure you use is correct for your battery type. Become familiar with the manufacturer's recommendations for recharging your batteries.

Explosive Gas: Hydrogen, **an explosive gas, may be discharged and collect in the area around a conventional 12V storage battery if not properly vented.** This problem is lessened with sealed batteries, but vented and liquid electrolyte batteries should be stored outside to avoid dangerous gas build up or acid spill in your radio shack.

Charging/Discharging Too Quickly: A lead-acid storage battery can overheat and give off flammable gas (hydrogen) or explode if it is charged or discharged too quickly. Check manufacturer's recommendations for charging and discharge rates, and utilize a manufacturer-recommended smart charger to adjust the charging voltage profile for AGM or gel cell type lead-acid batteries. Battery explosions can be fatal to anyone nearby!

Shorting the terminals of a 12-volt storage battery can cause burns, fire, or an explosion. Be very careful to avoid any conductor contacting across the two battery terminals! Protect the battery terminals.

And beyond all that, do not play with your radio in the bathtub. Next we'll consider precautions when working with antenna towers, but first take a look at the questions associated with electrical safety, **Section 13.1.**

www.HamRadioSchool.com/tech_media

Safety

13.2 | **Antenna & Tower Safety**

" *The lofty pine is oftenest shaken by the wind; High towers fall with a heavier crash; And the lightning strikes the highest mountain. – Horace*

Although the ancient Roman poet probably wasn't a ham operator, Horace clearly knew a thing or two about hazards with antennas and towers. My amateur radio station is one of many with an antenna perched up in a lofty pine that is often shaken by the wind. Other stations more well accoutred than mine have high towers erected and maintained by safety conscious hams who seek to avoid a heavy crash and to mitigate a lightning strike! Here we shall learn some basic safety precautions with antennas and towers that all hams should know and heed.

Antenna Tower Safety involves understanding potential dangers associated with erecting, operating, and maintaining any type of tower, mast, or antenna, and taking proper precautions to avoid injury or damage.

Climbing antenna towers presents multiple hazards that can cause injury or death.

Hard Hat & Safety Glasses: Members of a tower work team should wear a hard hat and safety glasses at all times when any work is being done on the tower. Tools or other objects dropped from heights represent significant hazards for head and eye injury. A set of pliers through the skull or a screwdriver through an eye socket is a poor way to enhance your ham radio experience.

Photo: Perry Jager NØWMZ
Pictured: Dave Novotny WA6IFI

TOB01

Figure 13.3: Climbing Safety Gear Includes a Hardhat, Safety Glasses, & Climbing Harness

Climbing Harness: A good precaution to observe before climbing an antenna tower is to put on a climbing harness in addition to other safety gear such as safety glasses. A harness, properly attached to the tower structure, helps avoid accidental falls. Better to be strung up than flung down to the ground.

Observer: It is never safe to climb a tower without a helper or observer. In the case of an injury, a fall, or a complication on the tower an observer or helper can provide immediate assistance, first aid, or seek additional emergency help.

Erecting a Tower or Antenna must be done carefully and with consideration for surrounding obstacles.

Overhead Electrical Wires are deadly when contacted directly or indirectly with a conductor such as a metal tower or mast. **Look for and stay clear of any overhead electrical wires.**

Minimum safe distance from a power line: When installing an antenna of any type the minimum safe distance from a power line is a distance so that if the antenna falls unexpectedly, no part of it can come closer than 10 feet to the power wires. This is an important safety rule for any antenna system. All antennas will come down sometime, whether by intention or by accident. If your antenna comes down upon a power line or is blown into one, chances are your radio gear will be damaged and lethal power could be within easy reach of anyone encountering the downed antenna! Don't take the chance – keep your antenna away from power lines.

Utility Poles: Utility poles should not have antennas attached to them since the antenna could contact high-voltage power wires. Although it might seem like a convenient mast to use, the risk to life and equipment is not worth it. Additionally, power lines are common incidental RF emission source, inducing noise in your receiver. Just stay away from active utility poles.

Gin Pole: A gin pole, used to lift tower sections or antennas, can help avoid strain or injury of workers installing the tower or antenna. When using a gin pole keep in mind the same safe distance precautions from power lines as noted above.

Crank-Up Towers: *Crank up towers* are a great way to get a high performance antenna high in the air for a short time. These towers typically have mechanically lifted segments that telescope or raise up with a manual or motor-powered crank in a matter of minutes. They can be a real convenience in areas where permanent antenna structures are prohibited. However, **never climb a crank-up tower unless it is in the fully retracted position,** lowest to the ground. These portable or temporary towers may collapse or fall if climbed while extended, and if your fingers, arms, legs or other body parts are in the way as the crank-up collapses, you will be severely injured or killed by the collapsing parts if not from the fall and impact with the ground. *Remember, crank it down first!*

Grounding Towers and Antennas: It is good practice to protect against lightning strikes and the potential of lightning energy being routed into your radio shack by properly grounding your external antenna or tower.

Local Electrical Codes: Grounding requirements for amateur radio towers or antennas are established by local electrical codes. You should make sure that you comply with all local electrical codes with any antenna system or tower.

Grounding for Lightning: For towers, a proper grounding method is to use separate eight-foot long ground rods for each tower leg, bonded to the tower and also to each other. Tower ground wires installed for lightning protection should be short and direct. Sharp bends must be avoided. Usually, broad conductor strap, such as copper strap, is best for grounding connections since it

T0B07

T0B11

T0B08 T0B12 T0B10

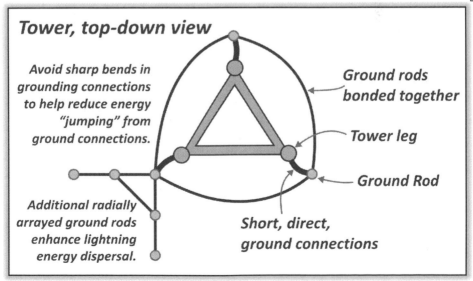

Tower, top-down view

Avoid sharp bends in grounding connections to help reduce energy "jumping" from ground connections.

Ground rods bonded together

Tower leg

Ground Rod

Additional radially arrayed ground rods enhance lightning energy dispersal.

Short, direct, ground connections

Figure 13.4: Top-down View of Tower Grounding Arrangement

provides greater surface area for current flow than wires. Sharp bends or creases in the grounding strap increase resistance and encourage lightning to depart from the conductor and "jump" to nearby objects.

Straight, direct, and short connections are best for lightning grounds, and don't skimp on the ground rods! They help dissipate the lightning energy into the earth when a strike occurs. Rods should be separated by 16 to 20 feet to promote lightning energy dispersal and to avoid saturating the ground with that energy – if the local surface ground cannot dissipate the lightning the energy will seek other routes to a ground level voltage, such as through your shack and equipment.

Coaxial Cable Feedline Lightning Protectors: Lightning protectors, also called *lightning tubes*, typically use common coaxial connector interfaces (N-connector or PL-259) so that they may be inserted in-line in coaxial antenna feedlines. If an electrical surge due to a lightning strike flows down the coax, the lightning tube is designed to break like a fuse very rapidly, significantly reducing the surge currents continuing down the coaxial feedline toward the shack and instead directing the energy safely to the ground.

Commonly such lightning protectors will be mounted and grounded onto a conductor plate (copper or aluminum) mounted on an external radio shack wall so that the plate may be easily grounded (See Figure 13.5). **All coaxial cable feedline lightning protectors should be grounded to a common plate which is in turn connected to an external ground** (such as an 8-foot or longer ground rod inserted into the earth). If you do not ground the protectors the lightning energy will not have a safe route to ground and may jump to other nearby conductors such as housing wires, pipes, computers, refrigerators, or anything conductive.

T0A07

With proper precautions you can survive even the worst antenna and tower calamities predicted by Horace and live to erect a better system another day. While most cases of simple wire or small vertical antenna erection present relatively little hazard, take no chances. Be certain of your environment and your local codes, always wear proper safety equipment, and always have an observer to assist you. Be safe, not sorry!

The questions! Practice the questions for **Section 13.2**.

www.HamRadioSchool.com/tech_media

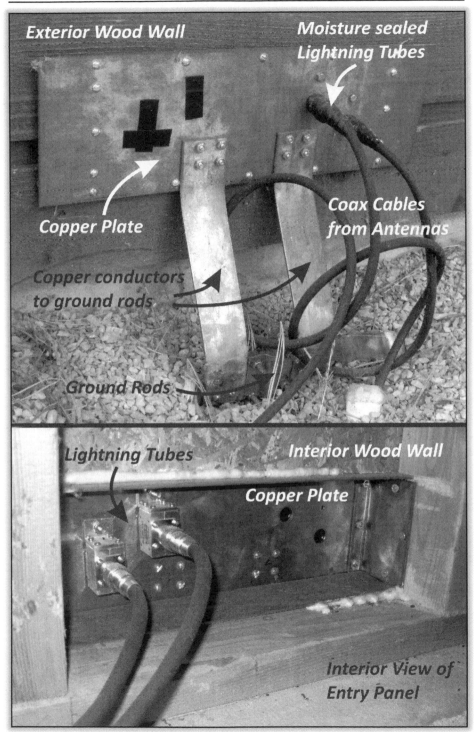

Figure 13.5: Lightning Protected Exterior Cable Entry Panel

13.3	Safety
	RF Exposure Safety

> **" It's not true I had nothing on, I had the radio on. – Marilyn Monroe**

Each time you push-to-talk, you expose yourself… to RF energy, I mean. And you are exposing others around you as well. How much radio exposure is safe? How do factors of frequency, power, or distance make a difference to exposure limits? How can you be sure your station is within safe limits? Should you put on aluminum foil coveralls before operating your station?

RF Exposure Safety involves understanding the FCC RF exposure limits and how to apply them with your station, ensuring that your station does not expose any person to levels of RF energy that exceed recommended levels. In most amateur stations RF exposure is not a great concern, but as an amateur operator you should be familiar with limits and requirements to evaluate exposure to assure safe operations for yourself, your family, and your neighbors.

Figure 13.6: Typical RF Aluminum Coveralls

Non-Ionizing Radiation: **UHF, VHF, and HF emissions are non-ionizing radiation.** This means that the RF emissions do not strip electrons from atoms like *ionizing radiation,* such as ultraviolet rays and X-rays. **As non-ionizing radiation RF radiation does not have sufficient energy to cause genetic damage** or biological molecular changes.

RF Heating of Tissues: RF emissions are absorbed by tissues in our body causing heating of those tissues. With excessive RF exposure tissue damage can occur due to the body's inability to dissipate the heat delivered. Think of the way a microwave oven works – a great amount of microwave RF energy is delivered inside the oven, rapidly cooking the items placed there that have no way of shedding the absorbed energy and resultant heat. Regarding the human body, a relative lack of blood flow to help dissipate excess heat makes our eyes and the male's testes most vulnerable to RF heating.

RF Burns: Just as you can be burned by infrared radiation that we perceive as heat, RF radiation of sufficient intensity can do the same. **RF burns are painful and may happen if a person accidentally touches your antenna while you are transmitting.** Unlike conventional heat burns, RF burns may extend deep below the skin surface and may require long healing times. RF burns are not a significant hazard with HT radios emitting 5W or less, but take care to ensure that no person touches your mobile or fixed station transmitting at higher power levels.

Power Density is the measure of RF power over area. Typically this is expressed as *milliwatts per square centimeter* (mW/cm^2). RF exposure limits recommended by the FCC, or the *Maximum Permissible Exposure* (MPE), are expressed in these units for each frequency band. Several factors affect power density and the resulting human exposure.

Factors Affecting RF Exposure: **Each of the following affect the RF exposure of people near an amateur station antenna:**

- **Frequency and power level of the RF field**
- **Distance from the antenna to a person**
- **Radiation pattern of the antenna**
- Duty Cycle of transmissions

Frequency: Exposure limits vary with frequency because the human body absorbs more RF energy at some frequencies than at others.

The greatest absorption, and thus **the lowest Maximum Permissible Exposure (MPE) limit,** is found for the VHF band of 30 to 300 MHz. **Note that this includes** the popular 2m band (near 144 MHz) and the 6m band **(near 50 MHz).**

Power Level: Greater power output increases the power density of the RF field. **The maximum power level that an amateur radio station may use at VHF frequencies** (1.25m, 2m, 6m bands) **before an RF exposure evaluation is required is 50 watts PEP at the antenna.** If you are outputting 50 watts with your transmitter you will likely have a little less than 50 watts at the antenna due to feedline loss. If your antenna is some distance above and away from people, you are safe. However, if you increase your power above 50 watts or if your antenna is nearby, such as inside your home or right outside the 2nd story bedroom, you must evaluate exposure levels.

PEP: *Peak Envelope Power* is the average power supplied to the antenna during an RF cycle at the peak of the amplitude of the RF signal's envelope. Most power meters have a PEP setting that allows an amateur operator to make measurements of PEP via a power meter on the feedline.

Distance from Antenna: RF energy spreads out as distance from the antenna increases, reducing the power per unit area. Specifically, power levels fall off as the square of the distance, so doubling the distance from the antenna reduces your exposure by a factor of four (1/4). Thus, **relocating antennas is one of the most common actions an amateur might take to prevent exposure to RF radiation in excess of FCC-supplied limits.**

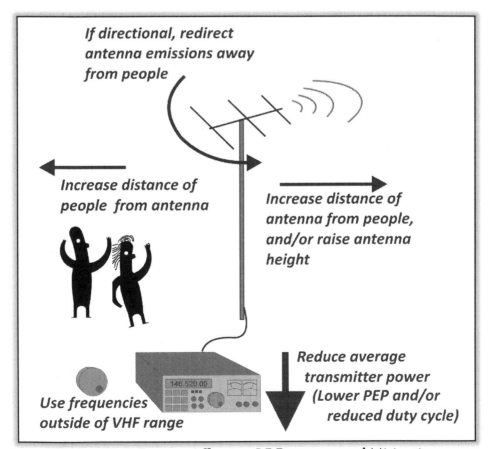

Figure 13.7: Factors Affecting RF Exposure and Mitigation

The duty cycle of transmission modes is determined by transmitter "on air" time and percent PEP within any single transmission. For 100% PEP modes (FM, CW) duty cycle is simply the ratio of "on air" time to total operating time. Multiple transmitter operating periods and receiver "listening periods" may comprise a standard averaging period of 6 or 30 minutes for estimating RF exposure levels.

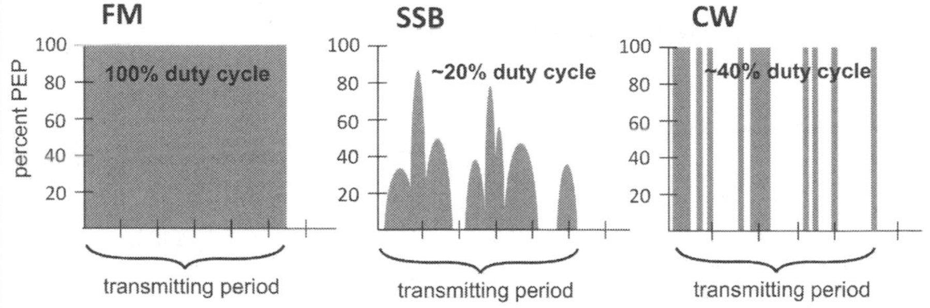

Figure 13.8: Duty Cycle of a Transmitter

Antenna Radiation Pattern: As we learned in Section 7.1, directional antennas will concentrate power in one direction, while isotropic antennas and dipole antennas distribute radiation more equally in all directions. Assessing RF exposure should take into consideration the power gain of any directional antennas used by the station.

Duty Cycle: Duty cycle affects the average exposure of people to radiation, so it is a factor used to determine safe RF radiation exposure levels. During an averaging time for RF exposure (6 or 30 minute measurement period), **duty cycle is the percentage of time that a transmitter is transmitting.** Thus, if the duty cycle is 50% across an averaging period, the power density may be doubled. **In a 6 minute averaging time, 2 times as much power density** (mW/cm^2) **is permitted if the signal is present for 3 minutes and absent for 3 minutes, rather than being present for the entire 6 minutes.** T0C10 T0C11 T0C13

More generally, duty cycle estimation should vary with the mode of transmission you are using. FM signals transmit at 100% power for the entire transmission time. SSB signals vary in power with your audio signal amplitude, dropping to near zero power between words and sentences, and causing the duty cycle to be reduced.

Complying with Limits: If your station requires an exposure evaluation, you may conduct it yourself or with help from a fellow amateur by any of the following **acceptable methods of determining compliance:** T0C06

- **By calculation based on FCC OET Bulletin 65**
- **By calculation based on computer modeling**
- **By measurement of field strength using calibrated equipment**

Note: **You can make sure your station stays in compliance with RF safety regulation by re-evaluating the station whenever an item of equipment is changed.**

Practical Advice on RF Exposure Compliance: Most new ham stations are not going to require an evaluation. But if you plan to use power levels above 50 watts (especially in 6m, 2m, and 70cm bands), if you plan to use a directional antenna with substantial gain figures, or if your antenna must be in close proximity with people, it is your responsibility to ensure your station is not exposing humans to RF levels in excess of the Maximum Permissible Exposure (MPE) limits defined in FCC OET Bulletin 65.

The FCC Office of Engineering and Technology (OET) Bulletin 65 from August 1997 contains more information than most new hams are likely to absorb in a short time. However, the tables and graph of MPE from the bulletin's appendix A is quite useful. Armed with a computed estimate of exposure in mW/cm^2 (milliwatts per square centimeter), you can use these tables to make a good estimate of whether or not your station is complying with MPE limits.

How can you easily make such a computation, you ask? The internet comes to the rescue! In addition to commercial and freeware computer software programs, several good internet sites are now available to estimate exposure levels using basic information that is easily known to you about your station and the exposure environment. Most of these sites utilize the formulas given in FCC OET Bulletin 65, but research sufficiently to be sure these are used. An internet search of "RF Exposure Calculator" will turn up multiple options. You will also find links to online exposure calculators in the Section 13.3 learning media at *HamRadioSchool.com*.

In most MPE calculator cases using the FCC formulas, you will need to enter the following types of information:

- **Average PEP** power at the antenna. This should be very close to your transmitter power, and you may measure close to your antenna with a power meter on the feedline. You may also need to adjust the power value for the duty cycle that is typical of your operational mode.

- **Gain** of your antenna in the direction of interest, or the isotropic gain.
- **Distance** to the area of interest for your measurement. That is, how far from your antenna to the living room or to your neighbor's house.
- **Frequency** of transmission, usually in MHz.

To use the FCC tables:

1. Make your estimates of exposure power density in mW/cm^2, perhaps using an online calculator as described earlier in this section.

2. Reference the frequency range in megahertz in the left column of the OET Bulletin 65 table (included at the end of this section):
   - For 6m and 2m bands the 30 – 300 MHz row applies.
   - For 70cm band the 300 – 1500 MHz row applies.
   - For 10m, the 3.0 – 30 MHz row applies.
   - Go across the rows to the Power Density column to read the MPE.

   Note that MPE for 6m and 2m is 1.0 mW/cm^2 for controlled exposure (you, the operator) and 0.2 mW/cm^2 for uncontrolled exposure (other people), and note that the other two ranges require a simple calculation based upon the specific frequency of exposure.

3. Compare your computed exposure level for your station with the MPE values in the table to determine if your station is exceeding the MPE.

4. If you find your station is exceeding the MPE, take steps to reduce the exposure.

Congratulations! You have completed all of the testable material for your FCC Technician VE Exam. Review the last set of questions from **Section 13.3**, take practice exams, and go get your license!

www.HamRadioSchool.com/tech_media

Please give us some feedback and let us know how you are doing by visiting the *HamRadioSchool.com* web site!

Good luck! I hope to hear you on the air soon. 73. WØSTU, clear.

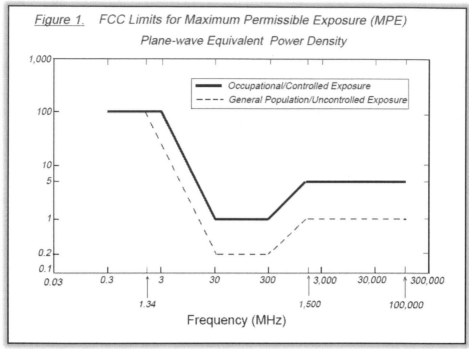

Figure 1. FCC Limits for Maximum Permissible Exposure (MPE) Plane-wave Equivalent Power Density

Figure 13.9: OET Bulletin 65 Chart of MPE (mW/cm²) by Frequency

Table 1. LIMITS FOR MAXIMUM PERMISSIBLE EXPOSURE (MPE)

(A) Limits for Occupational/Controlled Exposure

Frequency Range (MHz)	Electric Field Strength (E) (V/m)	Magnetic Field Strength (H) (A/m)	Power Density (S) (mW/cm^2)	Averaging $|E|^2$, $|H|^2$ or S (minutes)
0.3 - 3.0	614	1.63	(100)*	6
3.0-30	1842/f	4.89/f	(900/f^2)	6
30-300	61.4	0.163	1.0	6
300-1500	--	--	f/300	6
1500-100,000	--	--	5	6

(B) Limits for General Population/Uncontrolled Exposure

Frequency Range (MHz)	Electric Field Strength (E) (V/m)	Magnetic Field Strength (H) (A/m)	Power Density (S) (mW/cm^2)	Averaging $|E|^2$, $|H|^2$ or S (minutes)
0.3-1.34	614	1.63	(100)*	30
1.34-30	824/f	2.19/f	(180/f)*	30
30-300	27.5	0.073	0.2	30
300-1500	--	--	f/1500	30
1500-100,000	--	--	1.0	30

f = frequency in MHz   *Plane-wave equivalent power density

NOTE 1: *Occupational/controlled* limits apply in situations in which persons are exposed as a consequence of their employment provided those persons are fully aware of the potential for exposure and can exercise control over their exposure. Limits for occupational/controlled exposure also apply in situations when an individual is transient through a location where occupational/controlled limits apply provided he or she is made aware of the potential for exposure.

NOTE 2: *General population/uncontrolled* exposures apply in situations in which the general public may be exposed, or in which persons that are exposed as a consequence of their employment may not be fully aware of the potential for exposure or can not exercise control over their exposure.

Figure 13.10: FCC OEM Bulletin 65 Table of MPE Limits

Index of Terms

Element 2 Technician Exam Pool Question and Page Index

Continued...

EL. T5				EL. T7		
T5A01	128	T5D01	131	T6C01	149	T7A01	97	T7D01	139
T5A02	133	T5D02	131	T6C02	149, 158	T7A02	9	T7D02	139
T5A03	128	T5D03	131	T6C03	158	T7A03	95	T7D03	140
T5A04	128	T5D04	132	T6C04	155, 159	T7A04	185	T7D04	139
T5A05	128	T5D05	131	T6C05	155, 159	T7A05	83	T7D05	140
T5A06	128	T5D06	131	T6C06	150	T7A06	104	T7D06	142
T5A07	129	T5D07	131	T6C07	151	T7A07	13	T7D07	141
T5A08	129	T5D08	131	T6C08	149	T7A08	90	T7D08	160
T5A09	128	T5D09	131	T6C09	156	T7A09	79	T7D09	160
T5A10	133	T5D10	131	T6C10	150	T7A10	10	T7D10	141
T5A11	128	T5D11	131	T6C11	155	T7A11	97	T7D11	140
T5A12	63, 128	T5D12	132	T6C12	149			T7D12	139
				T6C13	149	T7B01	23		
T5B01	143	EL. T6				T7B02	178		
T5B02	66	T6A01	149	T6D01	157	T7B03	178		
T5B03	143	T6A02	149	T6D02	156	T7B04	180		
T5B04	142	T6A03	149	T6D03	156	T7B05	181		
T5B05	146	T6A04	149	T6D04	156	T7B06	182		
T5B06	144	T6A05	149	T6D05	156	T7B07	180		
T5B07	66	T6A06	150	T6D06	156	T7B08	182		
T5B08	144	T6A07	150	T6D07	151	T7B09	183		
T5B09	136	T6A08	156	T6D08	157	T7B10	23		
T5B10	137	T6A09	156	T6D09	148	T7B11	180		
T5B11	137	T6A10	145	T6D10	158	T7B12	182		
T5B12	66	T6A11	144	T6D11	157				
T5B13	66			T6D12	123	T7C01	112		
		T6B01	153			T7C02	119		
T5C01	149	T6B02	151			T7C03	118		
T5C02	149	T6B03	153			T7C04	120		
T5C03	150	T6B04	153			T7C05	120		
T5C04	150	T6B05	153			T7C06	120		
T5C05	63	T6B06	151			T7C07	124		
T5C06	63	T6B07	151			T7C08	119		
T5C07	63	T6B08	155			T7C09	124		
T5C08	133	T6B09	151			T7C10	124		
T5C09	134	T6B10	154			T7C11	124		
T5C10	133	T6B11	155			T7C12	123		
T5C11	134	T6B12	154			T7C13	113		
T5C12	118, 130								
T5C13	118, 130								

Made in the USA
San Bernardino, CA
02 October 2017